RED HOT CHILI PEPPERS

INSIDE THE VEINS OF
THE VELVET GROOVE

THE UNAUTHORISED BIOGRAPHY

MARTIN ROACH

ABOUT THE AUTHOR

Martin Roach gained a degree in Historical Research before starting his own publishing company, I.M.P. in 1992. Since then he has penned over 80 works on music, youth culture, celebrity and fi lm. Editions of his work have been sold to the USA, France, Germany, Italy, Czechoslovakia, Slovenia, Croatia, Australia, New Zealand, Belgium, Norway, Holland, South Africa, Japan, Canada, Hong Kong, UAE and Brazil.

He lectures on, and has written numerous articles, essays and critiques about, music, songwriting, pop and youth culture (including So You Want To Be A Pop Star and NME Top 100 Singles). He has been invited to talk on scores of radio and television shows including BBC 2, ITV, BBC Radio 1, 2, 4 and 5, Xfm, countless regional BBC and commercial stations and many print media interviews. In 1999 he undertook a three week promotional tour of the USA and Europe to support his Dr Martens book.

Martin Roach has to date written biographies of: White Stripes (Chrome Dreams 2003) Coldplay, The Strokes, Eminem, Korn, Limp Bizkit, Marilyn Manson, Manic Street Preachers, Destiny's Child, Radiohead, Madonna, REM, Jennifer Lopez, Kid Rock, Nirvana, Pearl Jam, Primal Scream and Nine Inch Nails.

RED HOT CHILI PEPPERS

Inside The Veins Of
The Velvet Groove

Martin Roach

RED HOT CHILI PEPPERS
Inside The Veins Of The Velvet Groove

By Martin Roach

A CHROME DREAMS PUBLICATION

First Edition 2004

Published By Chrome Dreams
PO BOX 230
New Malden
Surrey
KT3 6YY
UK
www.chromedreams.co.uk

ISBN 1 84240 220 X

Editorial Director   Rob Johnstone and Michael O'Connell
Editor   Rob Johnstone
Cover and interior design   Mark Fuks

funk

'Funk' is a term associated with the music of the Seventies, Eighties and beyond. Yet the concept of funk – and the original meaning of the word – goes back a lot further than this. The term is actually an intellectual word first recorded as Oxford University slang, and stretching back to 1677. In this year (or possibly earlier – it is not definite when the book was originally compiled) Junius's *Etymologicum Anglicanum* – a history of English words and phrases – lists the meaning of the word 'funk' as a state of fear or panic. The word probably comes from an old French word 'fonck', meaning agitation or distress. This is the meaning that is first referred to in 1743. By 1843, the phrase 'in a blue funk' – familiar still today – was in common usage, and the word also could be used to mean to flinch, or shrink away in fear. Another usage of the word – and this is where its use in music is derived – is of a strong smell. Again coming from an old French word listed as far back as 1633, 'funkier' meant to smoke, or to give off smoke. From this came the word 'funky,' which developed the meaning 'to give off a bad smell.' American English speakers adopted this meaning of the word, and by the end of the nineteenth century it appears to have been in common usage among both black and white English speakers in the USA to mean a musty smell. It is used at around the end of that century in the title of a tune by Buddy Bolden called 'Funky Butt'. 'Funk,' in the sense of a musty smell, then came to be used predominantly in the black community to describe that particular little musty scent exuded by someone engaged in physically demanding sexual acts, and came to be used in the language of jazz some time in the mid 1950s.

punk

'Punk' as a word stretches right back to the Algonquian tribe of Delaware, and – like 'funk' – stretches right back to the mid-seventeenth century at least. The Native American word 'ponk' means, literally 'living ashes.' The word developed in American English therefore, rather than in Europe, and soon came to refer to a pile of slow burning wood, or other such material, that could be used for setting light to fires. The term was developed in usage to refer to any kind of small pile of rubbish, and thus to describe worthless items or nonsensical ideas. In *The Story of a Bad Boy* published in 1869, the word has been coined to describe troublesome young hoodlums – the original punk kids. The word was first used in pop music in 1971 – well before the Ramones and Television in America and the Sex Pistols and Clash in the UK adopted it.

'punk-funk' or 'funk-punk'

Can be literally translated as a worthless kid who smells of the sex he has just had.

CHAPTER 1

The very first day of November, 1962 was when Anthony Kiedis spilled out into the world. He shared his birthday with the renowned Italian sculptors Cellini and Canova, as well as L.S. Lowry, the English artist. The charts in the pre-Beatles US (the Fab Four were still in Hamburg) were filled with artists such as Elvis, Neil Sedaka, Sam Cooke and Johnny Mathis while only three months previously, Marilyn Monroe had been found dead by her housekeeper, an empty bottle of sedatives nearby. American families were being actively encouraged to build their own nuclear shelters. Under the banner of 'A New Urgency – Big Things To Do', US families were reassured that if they took the right precautionary steps, in the event of a nuclear strike by the Reds, only 30% of the population would die in an instant. All very pertinent as when Anthony was born the world was still gripped by the Cuban missile crisis – and waiting to hear if Armageddon could be averted. This was the classic era of the Cold War, Russki-baiting, starched shirts, debut satellites, pop art and *The Beverly Hillbillies*. By the end of the year, Garth Brooks, k.d. Lang, Jon Bon Jovi, Jodie Foster and Tom Cruise would also been have born.

The Kiedis family home was in Grand Rapids, an exciting sounding name for a decidedly ordinary town. It was a predominantly Dutch area of Michigan and the Kiedis home was in a lower-middle-class area of the town. Anthony's mother was a secretary at a local law firm. His dad Jack Kiedis was an aspiring actor/screenwriter/filmmaker who would eventually go on to have supporting roles in films such as *Lethal Weapon* and *Doctor Detroit* as well as TV parts in shows such as *Starsky And Hutch* and *Night Court*. His doting mom Peggy was a less flamboyant personality than her husband, and she instilled in her young son the virtues of respect and compassion.

This humane trait was apparent very early on. Anthony's primary education was at a school known locally for accepting deaf and mentally disabled children. The boisterous Anthony became a self-appointed defender of these more vulnerable classmates, in the process earning himself many detentions and punishments for fighting. "I always got expelled for getting in fights with kids who'd torment the handicapped kids," he told one reporter. "And my mother was always OK with it. It was important to know somebody would stand behind me for doing what I believed in."

Although much is made in the media of his father's liberal approach to parenthood, his mother was equally influential. Both parents bequeathed on Anthony what he calls "the gift of being in love with life." Anthony has three siblings – two sisters: the youngest sister, Jennifer, often goes to Lakers games with Anthony while the elder sister, Julie, works as a writer in San Diego.

His father split up from this mother (they divorced in 1968) when Anthony was only one. For the first eleven years of his life, Anthony lived with his mother and enjoyed a very stable and loving home life. The 'normality' of his first eleven years with his mom is hard to ignore – though it shouldn't be seen as inferior to the wilder times he would later enjoy at his father's.

Despite being apart, Anthony admitted to cherishing the time he spent with his father. "Whenever I would go to visit him, I looked at it as if I was going to visit a superhuman person because, when we were together, the love was so concentrate... Since I didn't live with him, I didn't become aware of his terribly human traits until later than I may have otherwise."

His father's creative streak extended beyond the stage and to his approach to parenthood. He would mail Anthony love beads, posters of Bob Dylan, band T-shirts and so on, little bundles of alternative lifestyle piercing the sometimes suffocating cultural void that was typical Midwestern USA in the mid-Sixties. Under the assumed stage name of Blackie Dammett, Anthony's dad would arrive wearing snakeskin platform shoes, techni-coloured suits, long hair and an extravagant handlebar moustache. At times it was as if an alien had landed and Anthony adored him.

He would see him often and for long periods during summer holidays, when Blackie would regale him with anecdotes from Hollywood, audition tales and showbiz gossip. A wide-eyed young man from a Midwest town naturally found these sporadic ventures into the glitzy world of LA utterly compelling.

To her immense credit, Anthony's mother was acutely aware that her son was craning to experience life outside of Grand Rapids. She knew the attraction he felt to the stories he was hearing from California and, with no concern for the emotional cost to herself, she decided to send him west to live with his father in LA. It was to prove, arguably, the most momentous decision in the young Anthony's life.

So, just as Anthony was heading towards his pubescence, he uprooted and headed west to California. The difference in lifestyles between the Midwest and the West Coast could not have been greater. This was a world of celebrity, of partying 'til dawn, of waitresses/actresses serving you every night, Tinsel Town and the Hollywood dream. How could a pre-teen kid not be excited?

Everything changed when he went to live there. Blackie Dammett was handsome, confident and a sparkling socialite. His house was a very popular meeting place for all manner of actors, actresses, singers, writers and bohemian characters. People would arrive unannounced wearing outlandish costumes, bizarre hairstyles and clutching the latest record/novel/film concept etc which would invariably be pored over before the partying commenced. Blackie always avidly encouraged Anthony to join in the artistic conversations, read books, listen to music and generally soak up the cultural ambience.

Anthony gleefully admitted to *Rolling Stone* that, "to me, it just seemed like I'd landed in this magical kingdom where anything was possible. I got stoned, and my father had a girl over at the house, and she didn't have her shirt on. I said to myself, you know, 'How lucky could a boy be?' At the time, I thought I was the luckiest kid on the block." He later called these years "anarchy on a plate".

Anthony's much-documented enthusiasm for a healthy sex life began here. His father had a constant stream of beautiful girlfriends, as he tried to satiate a bacchanalian ambition to date all the world's most gorgeous women. This inevitably impacted on Anthony who was around models, actresses and other confident, attractive women from a very early age when most boys are still arguing about who has got the fastest bicycle. Anthony lost his virginity at the tender age of only twelve to a female friend of his dad's. He was enjoying a crash course in sexual education that no textbook or fumbling biology teacher could provide.

It wasn't just sex and partying that Anthony experienced. Life with Blackie also introduced him to the world of films. His father's own career as an actor may never have rivalled his son's latterday musical profile, but being surrounded by people in the movies made a big impression on Anthony. Indeed, when he was only fourteen, Anthony's father helped him secure very small roles in a couple of low-profile films, where he appeared under the tongue-in-cheek pseudonym Cole Dammett. A star on the walk of fame was hardly about to fall in his lap however – even what appeared to be a break in the form of a role as Sylvester Stallone's son in *F.I.S.T.*, proved to be a disappointment. Anthony had three words of script – "pass the milk" – and only his arm was visible in frame when he spoke. That same year he won a role as a weird kid/future Nazi in *The Boys From Brazil* alongside Gregory Peck and Laurence Olivier. Nonetheless, these small roles may have already justified his mother's decision to send him to LA – after all, it's doubtful he would still have been in 'the movies' if he was a fourteen-year-old still living in Grand Rapids.

Anthony's first draw on a joint was also with his dad; he started experimenting with drugs at the age of fifteen; it wasn't just showbiz, sex and drugs he encountered either – inevitably rock and roll was lurking in the corners too. So it was that Anthony was listening to The Eagles' *Hotel California* while his peer group were salivating over early disco or boy bands. "[That record] is heavily steeped in memories for me... I used to listen to [it] constantly," he says. "That brings back a lot of memories, mostly good, from that era. Randy Newman's 'I Love LA' is something they play at the Los Angeles Lakers basketball arena when the Lakers are walloping their opponent. So that also has good memories for me."

It wasn't just listening to rock and roll that got him hooked either. One of his former girlfriends had started dating Sonny Bono, who at the time was one of the biggest stars in the world and one of the luminaries of the West Coast scene. Sonny was naturally a very impressive figure to the pre-teen Anthony and subsequently proved to be a strong influence on the future Chili Pepper. At the time, the singer was still reeling from the acrimonious break-up of his high-profile marriage to Cher, so this was altogether a celebrity-Hollywood baptism of fire for Anthony. This was not your average middle-class childhood.

While millions of other young men were being brought up in households where returning home late at night smelling of a few Budweisers is tantamount to social rebellion, Anthony, unsurprisingly, *loved* living with his father. He worshipped him, later telling *Rolling Stone* that, "My first hero was my father... he was very significant in my mind... He was incredibly enthusiastic about fatherhood and teaching me a condensed, boiled down super-intense version of everything that he had learned in his life. So I would get these high-concentration lessons of culture and love and would walk away just reeling and rocking. I remember saying to myself, 'That guy is deep.' Even as a toddler I had that sensation that he was different. He was my dad, my hero. That lasted for a very long time." Anthony openly credits his father for opening up what he calls "a seed of creativity" that changed his life forever. "He taught me that it was OK to think and be and act and invent differently."

Thus, by the time Anthony was just old enough to get married, he had already experienced most of the rites of passage that young men face, and then some. With the benefit of hindsight, if anyone was going to be a rock star, it was Anthony. Even if he'd been able to sit down with a copy of *Spinal Tap* at that time and get an idea of what goes on, he was already experienced way beyond his years and didn't have much to learn about life in showbiz.

Sixteen-year-old Anthony was so fired up with confidence and zest for life that he even started to rebel against his father, the man who in many ways had helped imbue those qualities in the young Kiedis. By his own admission, Anthony started to question his father as his perfect hero: "It wasn't a bursting of my illusion bubble, it was more that I was becoming jaded from the information that I was receiving on a daily basis. As I became more information-bound, I started to see him as more ordinary and I realized that other people had great concepts as well. And there was just a need to say 'fuck you', as well… It was time to rebel and find new heroes." Anthony moved out of his father's home, taking a room in a shared house.

It has been suggested that such a liberal childhood where the normal parameters of social acceptability were stretched to the limit on a daily basis may have infected Anthony with a craving for the darker side of life. If that's true, it would prove to be a craving that would have devastating consequences later on in his life.

Anthony attended Fairfax High in Hollywood, which boasted among its list of illustrious former pupils none other than super-producer Phil Spector, master songwriter Jerry Lieber and Herb Alpert. Also studying at that time was a young man who would come to be one half of the Red Hot Chili Peppers and one of Anthony's closest friends in life: Flea.

CHAPTER 2

Melbourne, Australia, the capital of Victoria state, built on goldrushes and the river Yarra. As far from the LA metropolis that spewed forth the Chili Peppers as it is possible to get but the birthplace nonetheless of Michael Balzary, a.k.a. Flea (born two weeks before Anthony Kiedis on October 16, 1962), the long-term equal partner with Anthony in the band's eventful story. Like his future funk-soulmate, Michael was the product of a broken marriage – his parents divorced when he was just five. And, like Anthony, he resided with his mother, who relocated thousands of miles to live in New York and then, briefly, in Los Angeles.

It was here that Michael's mother re-married, having met and fell in love with respected jazz musician Walter Urban Junior. As well as picking up the nickname Flea, Michael also picked up a fascination with jazz and funk from his step-father Walter. It was a fiery relationship with Walter – despite gelling with Flea quickly and strongly, his step-father was frequently in brushes with the law, many of which were violent and, as Flea revealed later in life, often involved guns.

The household was short of cash but never short of inspirational guests. Walter invited scores of brilliant musicians around and Flea could not avoid becoming obsessed with the people, the characters, the names and above all, the music they played. Even before he was in his teenage years, Flea had started to jam with his father's peer group when they regularly came around to play through the night. At first he mainly played the trumpet, becoming so proficient that he was quickly awarded the first trumpet chair in the Los Angeles Junior Philharmonic Orchestra. He was awarded a scholarship to assist in paying fees for private tuition – with formal training added to natural ability, Flea soon became a very talented musician indeed.

However, it was not in the hushed stands and formal dress of the classical world where Flea's fascination with music lay. His appetite for jazz, classical, be-bop and – increasingly – funk seemed insatiable. While his school friends were listening to disco and dance-floor hits, Flea was poring over old vinyl by the likes of Miles Davis, Ornette Coleman and Dizzy Gillespie.

Again, like Anthony over at Blackie Dammett's house, Flea was fortunate enough to come in to contact with celebrity at a young age. One night, backstage at a Gillespie gig, Flea's mother introduced him to the legendary trumpet player and the two chatted together for over fifteen minutes. The following weeks saw nothing but Gillespie on Flea's modest bedroom turntable. Yet increasingly, the jazz pioneers found themselves filed behind the growing collection of funk records in Flea's bedroom boxes.

When Flea had been a toddler, his parents were concerned about his chronic shyness, but as he developed into a teenager, complete with an accomplished musical ability and ever-increasing spectrum of musical knowledge, his confidence grew. By the time he enrolled at Fairfax High School, he had blossomed into a very confident and individual character.

That said, his unusual musical tastes alienated him from his peer group, as did his odd accent and unorthodox fashion sense, so that he was regularly picked on (one kid who often derided Flea for his record collection was called Jack Irons, but more on him later). By way of escape, Flea simply returned home as fast as he could each night and ensconced himself in his bedroom with the legends of jazz and funk for company.

In the school-yard, Anthony Kiedis was busy keeping the peace one day when he broke up a fight between one of his friends and an unusual looking boy. He found himself standing opposite Flea. Despite this awkward first meeting, Flea and Anthony instantly became friends, sharing a similarly disjointed early childhood, an obsession with music and a fierce refusal to slot into the accepted 'jock' culture of American high schools. They quickly earned a reputation for being anarchic and free spirits, much to the disdain of their teachers and the bemusement of their classmates.

One anecdote from this time recounts how Anthony and Flea developed a penchant for jumping from tall buildings into swimming pools, but goes on to detail how the former misjudged his leap one day and cracked into the poolside one day, fracturing his back in the process. Quite how this serious injury does not deter him from being the frenetic frontman of the Chili Peppers remains a mystery!

Another pastime was the rather more sedate hobby of walking through Yosemite nature reserves in northern California, where they would apparently hike around the countryside for days on end. As Flea put it, "I think there were times when Anthony and I were all each other had." Many years later, when the Red Hot Chili Peppers were one of the biggest bands on the planet – indeed of all-time – this feeling of spiritual and personal closeness had not dissipated one iota: "Flea and I were made to affect each other," said Anthony in 2002. "We are almost too close and too much one and the same to even talk sometimes. When Flea cries I cry and when Flea smiles it makes me smile."

Flea was renowned for his encyclopaedic musical knowledge and ability and it was perhaps inevitable that pretty soon his talents would be sought after by the usual tranche of bands. In high school, one such outfit was called Chain Reaction, the brainchild of a duo by the name of Hillel Slovak and Flea's erstwhile tormentor, Jack Irons (born 18 July, 1962, the only Californian native of the early Chilis. Haifa (Israel)-born Hillel (31 March, 1962) was yet another future Chili Pepper who came from a broken home – when his parent's marriage disintegrated, he moved to Los Angeles too but retained a fierce pride in his home country. "He was very proud of his heritage," remembered Flea years later. "He was also a wild partyer. Before he got carried away with the drugs, he was a lot of fun. He was really funny and kind of funny looking. Real skinny with a long head and big lips."

Jack and Hillel were bosom buddies at Fairfax High and didn't need to ask each other if they fancied forming a band. Their inspiration was Kiss, whose bizarre brand of make-up and metal was selling tens of millions of records every year. The duo's first efforts were a ropey Kiss mime act that soon evolved in to playing Jimi Hendrix covers too. This was due to Hillel's growing fascination with Hendrix, whose unique guitar-playing was arguably the biggest single influence on the young musician. Their very first band was the aforementioned Chain Reaction, who aside from covering Hendrix also aspired to being a bizarre cross between Led Zeppelin and Queen!

Hillel had befriended Anthony at Fairfax and naturally Jack Irons got to know the future Chilis singer too. Through Anthony, Flea was introduced into the mix and there, albeit in fledgling form and not even so much as a band, were future founding members of the Red Hot Chili Peppers.

The first group they all formed together was christened Los Faces but that was as far as it went, with no gigs ever being played – it was more of a social circle really, a funk/punk frat house so to speak. Though they weren't yet playing together, the early Eighties were spent hanging out together, listening to the sounds blasting out of boom boxes in the parking lots of local venues like The Starwood. The Starwood was one of the few venues that not only tolerated but also celebrated the new wave of bands and the visionaries, fuck-ups and freaks they attracted. LA is a city that thrives on drama – throw in a bunch of highly-strung youngsters fuelled on booze, speed, acid and it made for some interesting and colourful nights out.

The cluster of future Chilis became increasingly tightly-knit, with beer, sex, drugs and women and music being the shared interests. It was here that Anthony first dubbed them "the four motherfuckers from Fairfax". They later talked of this camaraderie as 'The Fax City 4', an idea taken from *Judge Dredd*.

With a new name – Anthym – and a new determination to forge something special, the four friends' first real band began at the turn of the Eighties. Flea was, oddly, asked to play bass, even though he had never done so before – but his accomplished trumpet work and detailed technical knowledge as well as his library of funk/soul records meant that he was a natural fit for the instrument that more than any other came to define the Chilis' sound. Within weeks, his bass playing was turning heads. Witnesses to the embryonic Anthym describe the band as 'garage punk' but that was spiced up considerably every time Flea developed something new on the four string. Some reports suggest that Hillel was an active teacher of the bass for Flea at this time.

One of the band's biggest followers was Anthony, who never missed a gig as the trio started to work the local circuit. At first he was keen to chip in as much as he could so he took to announcing the band's arrival on stage. Anthony remembered for MTV how he used to introduce them: "Cal Worthington calls them the hottest rockers in LA. Their parents call them crazy, and girls call them all the time. But I call them like I see them, and I call them… ANTHYM!"

Aside from his love of music, Anthony was an avid fan of drama and acting at Fairfax too (in this sphere he was actively encouraged by his high school English teacher Mrs Vernon who also prodded him into creative writing). Perhaps not surprisingly, it wasn't long before he became far more involved, jumping up on stage to rant self-penned poetry and act as an oddball MC to rather bemused audiences. Meanwhile, he was drawing inspiration from the box-fresh sounds of hardcore and hip-hop, then in it's embryonic stage, and it was this new ingredient to the mix that immediately started to separate the inexperienced band from their peers. Rap, for Anthony, opened up a whole new world, as he told *Rolling Stone*'s David Fricke magazine: "Hearing Grandmaster Flash and the Furious Five, he says, "gave me the notion that I could do something musically without being Marvin Gaye."

By the time punk rock fully emerged snarling and spitting in 1977, Los Angeles was ready for a shake up. As the blackened heart of American music, like London, in the early-to-mid-Seventies the LA music scene was still clinging to Sixties styles but had replaced all notions of peace and love with indulgence and excess – in life and in music. Two pivotal events turned the Sixties sour and both took place in California – the brutal killing of a Rolling Stones fan by bikers at a show in Altamont and, just as notorious, the Charles Manson Family murders in the upper-middle-class neighbourhoods of LA. A drifter, career con and struggling musician, Manson and his glassy-eyed followers lived out in the dusty wilds of Death Valley, but were often to be seen on the fringes of the LA music scene. Manson cast a long shadow over the city in the preceding decade. For many he merely confirmed what they had already suspected: behind the sunshine and enviable lifestyle, the glitz and the glamour (which the young Anthony Kiedis was gleefully exploring), Los Angeles was a place capable of great darkness – and the twin playgrounds of the music and film industries were far from immune.

As the Seventies progressed and the naiveté of the peace-loving Sixties dissipated, LA's music scene become increasingly fuelled by cocaine behind the scenes, and what some observers saw as an overblown sense of importance within its biggest stars of the day – Aerosmith and Fleetwood Mac for example. Musicians wore beards, travelled in limos and were indulged by all-comers so long as their records were still selling. Their lives were so decadent and detached, to the kid on the street they might as well have come from another planet. Something had to change.

And change it did. For all its wealth and assumed sense of hipness, Los Angeles was a relative late starter in the punk rock wars. New York and London had long been viewed as the two cities that spawned the first wave of punk bands – though the proto-punk band The Stooges came from Ann Arbour, Michigan and had their sound rooted in the Sixties (the Chili Peppers would later cover their incendiary anthem 'Search & Destroy'). On his legendary LA show 'Rodney On The Roq' - inspired by Iggy Pop, the New York Dolls, the anything-goes aesthetic attitude of Bowie and new sounds by The Ramones and Sex Pistols - the KROQ DJ Rodney Bingenheimer was showcasing a new subculture emerging in the City Of

Angels, a musical environment that had no place within the limo and coke scene of the West Coast.

The first punk-inspired bands to emerge in the city were centred around the Sunset Strip and the odd seedy little performance space – bands such as X, The Runaways (featuring scene queen Joan Jett), The Go-Gos (featuring Belinda Carlisle), and more gonzo-sounding groups like The Dickies and Weirdos. From out of town came San Franciscans like Dead Kennedys, Crime, the Nuns and the Avengers, followed swiftly afterwards by proto-hardcore bands like Black Flag, whose SST label would significantly impact on alternative music in the Eighties. All of these bands were inspiring each other to stretch to new extremes. Punk rock was more than just a fashion-led movement - it was a groundswell of energy that inspired radical ways of living to match the garish attire that went with it. Punk rock was exciting, subversive dangerous and youth-based. Best of all it was against the liberal hippy ideals of the generation that had gone before – the generation currently dictating the terms in the music industry.

Pivotal in the birth and development of punk rock in Los Angeles were The Germs, who arrived on the scene in 1977 with a series of seminal shows. Led by enigmatic and doomed frontman Darby Crash, the band best epitomised the death-trip fixated LA underbelly, where drugs, art, music and sex collided. The Germs picked up followers among the disenfranchised, the angry and the lost souls of the city and its sun-drenched suburbs, like the affluent Orange County. Crash himself was enigmatic, articulate and a survivor of a troubled and unconventional upbringing. Along with Germs guitarist (and future Nirvana member) Pat Smear, he had attended a radical school where he had dabbled with acid, studied Christian Scientology and lived an unstructured academic life most pupils would dream of (different in specifics but equally liberal as Anthony's early years?). Crash's songs were nihilistic and The Germs' music was fast, short, dirty and barely listenable. Their live shows were legendarily raucous affairs, played in either traditional rock clubs of the Sunset Strip like The Roxy (which were often ended by the LAPD, who tended to treat the burgeoning young punks as sub-human scum) or short-lived, unlicensed spaces.

In 1977/78 punk rock in LA was as much a lifestyle choice as a musical movement. Being a punk guaranteed, at best, animosity from pseudo-hippies, jocks and 'straights' alike; at worst constant harassment from the cops and, quite often, unprovoked violence from those who felt threatened by a new sub-culture they knew nothing about, by music they would never understand.

Yet here for the first time, was a scene that welcomed all-comers (and in LA punk rock did attract its fair share of maniacs, dealers, hookers and older weirdos) and which didn't conform to the usual rules, the rules imposed by school, parents, by society, and by rock and roll itself. Mentally and spiritually, punk rock offered a place to those with nowhere to go.

Darby Crash's death at the age of twenty-two in 1980 made him a martyr to punks and he became as iconic a figure as Sid Vicious who had died of a drug overdose the year before. To a teenage Anthony Kiedis and Flea, The Germs were god-like. Their music was a brutally rendered expression of discontent that was highly appealing to anyone with too much energy, an active imagination and a rebellious streak. Like Flea, Crash – real name Paul Beheam - had come from a broken home and grown up a relatively poor boy amongst wealthier classmates, and like Kiedis he had a broad-minded upbringing which allowed him to dabble in drugs from a young age. The Germs and their contemporaries opened up a whole new world for Flea and Anthony – and in doing so opened up a sea of possibilities. Musicians like Mike Watt of the Minutemen and the Meat Puppets have carried the Germs' torch throughout their careers; Hole and Jane's Addiction performed and recorded Germs songs while an album *A Small Circle Of Friends: A Tribute to The Germs* surfaced in 1996 featuring a bizarre version of Germs favourite 'Media Blitz' by Flea himself.

"What punk rock was about me was never have to say you are sorry," explained Flea, who attended the band's final ever show at The Starwood in 1980. " I love The Germs. They were one of the best rock bands ever."

It was punk rock that first made the forming of a band possible. At the heart of the music was a do-it-yourself approach executed by the Ramones in New York, by the Sex Pistols and The Clash in London and picked up by The Germs and Black Flag, decreeing that if you don't like something, then take action. If high street fashion was tawdry, then subvert it. Literally, rip it up and create your own inimitable style. If you don't like the overblown pomposity of Led Zeppelin, then make your own noise. The core of punk rock was a youthful energy and general sense of irreverence that allowed bands like The Germs to make records, something the major labels would never have allowed, nor accepted. The idea that *anyone can do it* was what appealed to the two teenagers from Fairfax – jazz was great and so were The Beatles and Jimi Hendrix, but that shit took ability, something they were then-lacking. All punk required was a surplus of energy and a set of cast-iron balls.

Despite this shared fascination with funk and punk between Anthony, Flea, Jack and Hillel, it all came to a grinding halt just when it seemed they had something worth pursuing. Anthony had started a political science major at UCLA but that would not interfere with the band at all. However, Flea was approached to join seminal Eighties punksters, Fear, and he duly accepted the offer. Understandable perhaps, as that LA band had a considerable reputation, fired by the manic lead singer Lee Ving and backed up by chaotic live shows that were always outrageous, occasionally violent but never to be missed. Flea was only eighteen and found the enigmatic Ving something of a father figure, even though he did not agree with everything Ving said or believed in. With lyrics such as "steal the money from your mom, buy a gun/kill your mother and father", he always knew this was not going to be your average band.

Flea had already been diversifying anyway. His first acting role would come as disaffected punk Razzle in Penelope Spheeris's credibly and clearly directed punk alienation movie *Suburbia* (known as *The Wild Side* in the US). When he joined Fear, it seemed that the future Red Hit Chili Peppers' shared dreams were effectively still born.

Not so. After being apart for some time, the four friends were asked to play a guest slot at a gig at the local café De Grande venue, in their friend, Gary Allen's Rhythm Lounge Club night. Considering they were not actually a band at this point, it was a brave decision to accept the offer – not least because they only had one old bassline which Flea liked and some note pads with Anthony's poetry scribbled in them. The latter had by now adopted the temporary stage name of Antwan The Swan.

According to rumour, the band took a bagful of acid on the night of this gig and went on stage to produce a madcap yet fascinating set, topped off by the chosen moniker of Tony Flow And The Miraculously Majestic Masters Of Mayhem (no doubt not too easy to say when tripping on acid). The set consisted of a sole rendition of 'Out In LA', a poem written for to the city they loved, the city that would prove to be their muse over the following two decades.

Further gigs mainly at strip clubs and bars on Sunset Strip quickly fuelled the fire of record industry gossip – suddenly, the four motherfuckers from Fairfax had record companies sniffing around their digs. Any band that boasted influences such as the Germs, Black Flag, Fear, Minutemen, X, alongside Parliament-Funkadelic and Sly & the Family Stone had to be worth a look. This was 1983. One small problem was the convoluted name, but in typical fashion, the four mates all agreed to truncate it to something more manageable – the Red Hot Chili Peppers. To this day, they maintain they found the name on "a psychedelic bush in the Hollywood hills."

CHAPTER 3

At this point in the story, LA record biz veteran Lindy Goetz enters the fray. He was known by/knew of everybody in town and, having heard on the grapevine about the band, went to see them play live. After the show, he was sufficiently impressed to tell them he could secure them a record deal, but for now they should continue to gig and gig *hard*. In the meantime, they would periodically meet with Goetz for a catch-up, enjoying the free lunches and advice on offer as well as Goetz's obvious enthusiasm for their band. "We actually really liked Lindy," said Flea. "It wasn't like he was just a mark or anything, we were just hungry!"

Realising that they already had a buzz surrounding them, the Chilis duly started to gig frantically, sometimes every night. The venues they frequented were never far from the seedier side of life, such as Starwood. One rather more middle-class gig was their first ever out-of-town show, in upmarket Aspen. After their set was curtailed prematurely, the promoter sent them packing with a warning not to bring their "black music" back ever again to offend his clients.

It wasn't just a tour van that they all used together. They also shared digs, renting a "ghetto style" apartment on Hollywood Boulevard that all of them would live in at some point. On the surface, this party-loving foursome did not appear to be the ideal tenants and so it proved. At one point, their frustrated landlady, exasperated at the continued failure to pay rent, took off the apartment's door as an incentive to catch up on their arrears. The Chilis simply carried on living there rent-free, without a front door.

At this stage, they were gigging anywhere for anything, playing shows, partying through the night and looking – to the casual outside observer at least – like a band who genuinely didn't give a fuck what anyone else thought. Which was true.

It was around this time that the Chilis first performed in a 'costume' that would come to make/haunt their early career: stark naked except for a white tube sock over the penis. Simple, stylish, cold but, hey, they lived in LA where the sun always shined and a band wearing only socks over their genitals was nothing out of the ordinary.

The idea first cropped up back when Anthony was only seventeen and trying to dampen the amorous advances of an unwanted female admirer. She kept sending him letters with pornographic cards enclosed, often including a fold-out penis with a yardstick on it. When she turned up unannounced at his home one day, for some unspecified reason he chose to answer the door naked but for the cock-sock. "Not just over the cock, but over the cock and balls," Anthony helpfully explained. "It was just a gag. And it was a good gag." He also said, "[I] walked out to greet her as if nothing was different – casual, like a Monty Python episode. It was actually a great phallic look."

One night he recounted this tale with glee to his flat-mates and they in turn started to get drunk and prance around the flat naked but for the sock. It became just a silly prank, a bit of a party trick.

Then the band was booked to play a strip club called the Kit Kat, where curvaceous naked girls cavorted around the stage as they played. Perhaps understandably, most of the almost entirely male crowd watched the girls more than the punk-funk nutters on stage, and the Chilis were not best pleased. After playing a rather subdued set, they returned for the encore with only their genital socks on, to play a hilarious and rapturously received version of Hendrix's 'Fire'. Anthony remembers well how the adrenalin was coursing through his veins (probably one vein in particular) for this stunt. "Brother, let me tell you, when we came out of the little dressing room backstage, we were levitating with nervous energy. I could not find my feet on the stage... we just had this look in our eyes like we were from outer space." Crucially, someone in the strip club had a video camera and captured the moment on tape forever. Overnight, the Chili Peppers were the talk of the town. As a comical footnote, Flea tells the tale of how the manager of the strip club (filled with totally exposed women) ran up to them after their virtually naked encore shouting, "No pubes! I told you guys no pubes!"

Lindy Goetz would become the band's long-time manager and he recalls how the media attention on the cock-socks was out of proportion to the part it actually played, perhaps no more than fifteen per cent of shows. At one show in Vancouver, he told the wary police that the band were wearing G-strings to hold the socks in place: "They bought the story," Goetz remembers. "There's no wire. It's just a big sock off of their foot."

A residency at the Cathay Grand Club followed, as did yet more gigs. Although various members were still dabbling in other bands/projects, it was already clear that the Chilis had stumbled upon a unique chemistry. Remarkably, the word of mouth on the band was sufficiently strong during this chaotic period that EMI Records America offered them an eight album deal. It was only six months since their first ever show.

The problem was, they only had half a band. Although Flea had decided that the EMI deal was a signal to finally quit his work with Fear (and was more attractive than an offer to join John Lydon's PiL), two other members were not so certain. Jack and Hillel had formed another band, the short-lived What Is This? (really a continuation of Anthym), a highly appropriate name for a group that pulled in a bewildering array of influences, from punk to funk and everything in between. The band struggled to gather much of a following however (they would release one self-titled album before splitting up in 1985), but in the meantime, the Chili Peppers were severely weakened.

Worse still, Flea and Anthony could not even bring Hillel and Jack into the studio for sessions, as they were contracted to MCA for their work with What Is This? So, days after signing a record deal, the Red Hot Chili Peppers had to start scouting for new members to replace the missing half of the band. Meantime, they formulated a three-step masterplan for the band, which was only half a joke: make their debut album a masterpiece; accompany that with a watershed video; and support the album with a breath-taking tour.

The recruitment of new members was considerably pressurised by the fact EMI had (understandably) booked studio time and secured the services of a producer – Gang Of Four guitarist Andy Gill. While the future Chili Peppers were clearly enamoured with black funk music, it took the brash energy of punk rock to give them the confidence to play both sounds in their own unique way. They loved rock and funk equally and saw little differentiation between the two. Their approach was 'Why not?' and punk's central tenet of lack of ability and proficiency was just the confidence booster they needed. Somewhat ironically, it took four working class white men from the north of England to provide that extra inspiration. Gang Of Four rose to prominence after punk rock's first wave. With Margaret Thatcher at the helm, as the Seventies gave way to the Eighties, Britain ended a dark period of conservatism – in politics, in art and in pop music. It was left to fringe groups to kick against the right-wing mentality that had tainted 'Little England'. Gang Of Four were brutal and brittle, an intriguing combination of punk rock, tight fluid funk and well-informed leftish politics. At the centre of their sound was David Allen's bass riffs – after a decade of mindless disco and stripped-down punk, Gang Of Four were a rare band who you could dance to *and* think to. Their music appealed to a broad section of music fans and three thousand miles away from Leeds, Flea was painstakingly deconstructing Gang Of Four and learning to play along on his bass, night after night.

Many years later, during the Lollapalooza tour of 1992, Flea – already considered by many to be one of the best ever bassists in rock music – would later tell Allen that the punk-funk of Gang of Four's first two albums *Entertainment* and *Solid Gold* had taught him everything he knew about playing.

"Their first two albums were hugely influential records," Flea re-iterated to the BBC. "Gang Of Four are one of the finest bands that England has ever produced and, consciously or subconsciously, they have influenced a lot of things that we write. They had the English, white angst funk thing happening." But it would transpire that Flea couldn't get a relationship going with Gill.

It had seemed fortuitous when the duo quickly found guitarist Jack Sherman and drummer Cliff Martinez (formerly of Lydia Lunch 's 13.13, as well as Captain Beefheart's Band and The Weirdos). With Gill on board to bring the Gang Of Four's seminal funk-rock influence to the studio, the first step at least seemed within their grasp. Unfortunately, it was not to be and their eponymous debut album was a fairly turgid affair.

There were several reasons for this, not least the fact that Sherman and Martinez had been hastily thrust into a band that had a very particular musical vision and style, so it was asking a lot of anybody to blend seamlessly into the mix that quickly. For a band that prided themselves on their all-for-one brotherly attitude, losing half the team on the eve of recording their debut was potentially disastrous, not least because their music had certain intricacies that were only effective when played with precision. This was exacerbated severely by the Red Hot Chili Peppers' debilitating relationship with Andy Gill.

Listening to the Gang Of Four's back catalogue, the uncompromising sound, the political rhetoric and the dark, furious rhythms suggested that the energetic (albeit largely apolitical) ideas of the Chilis could only benefit. Add to this the fact that, as discussed, the Californian twosome in the Chilis were big fans of the Yorkshire act's innovative post-punk/funk hybrid and it is fair to say EMI seemed to have made a wise decision.

However, early on in the sessions it became clear that the personal chemistry was not ideal. Gill made it clear that he felt much of his recorded output with the Gang Of Four was "bought by a few lunatics" and he held little respect for that – to the Chilis, who were fans, this was most unsettling. Gill had also evolved away from the funk-punk that spliced so much of the Gang's work, and was decidedly more pop-oriented than the Chilis preferred. He had many disagreements with Flea and Anthony about where the album should be going, with talk of drum machines and pop causing near-terminal conflicts. Rumour has it that at one point Flea and Anthony were so disillusioned that they delivered Gill a human faeces in a pizza box on a mixing desk in LA's El Dorado Studios. When Gill finally came to suggest that they used a drum machine instead of Martinez they were in real difficulty.

Add to this tension the fact that, despite being accomplished musicians and fearsome live performers, the Chilis were novices in the recording studio. Gill himself was widely acknowledged as a studio wizard and a musical visionary but he had also not previously produced outside of the Gang Of Four. The environment to make that 'classic' debut album was never ideal.

'Classic' is not a word that can be used when talking about the Red Hot Chili Peppers' first album. In the album's own sleevenotes, Flea speaks of his disappointment that they hadn't made the debut masterpiece they'd spoken of, but he also goes on to highlight how a more philosophical Anthony reassured him that this was all part of the learning curve and that "had we been too good too fast we would never have continued the long and rich growing process we are still on." Flea has since said that although he has these reservations, "the record has some great moments." But you have to look pretty hard to find them.

That an inferior line-up of the Red Hot Chili Peppers recorded their debut album was obvious. As is evident, while this early version of the band was musically proficient and exuded a confidence in dipping in and out of various styles, the songs and the clean production just didn't have that bone-crunching power with which the Chili Peppers then-live show and latterday albums would become synonymous.

The original demos for the self-titled debut were produced by Spit Stix, drummer with Flea's erstwhile stage pals, Fear. The demos also featured Hillel and Jack shortly before they left the ranks for What Is This?, and the tapes – albeit crudely formed – suggest that this album could have been a much stronger record. The songs in demo stage that would later be included as bonus tracks on the album re-issue, were more vibrant, alive and raucous than some of the final versions that made it to the album… and infinitely better for it.

Talking to the press, Anthony uttered this now-famous quote which magically summed up what the very early Chili Peppers were about: "What we originally set out to do was to be complete and utter perpetrators of hardcore, bone-crunching mayhem sex things from heaven," he remarked. "To try and describe that to another musician, and have it mean something, is nearly impossible unless you've grown up with that person." The same could perhaps be said for the songwriting split between the tracks compiled with Jack and Hillel as against those written with Martinez and Sherman – note the energy in 'Police Helicopter' and 'Green Heaven' compared to the banality of 'Buckle Down'.

Announcing the band's funk-heavy sound on record for the first time, 'True Men Don't Kill Coyotes' was a strutting, staccato song that took the listener on a journey through the Hollywood hills with references to riding 'sabre-tooth horses' and 'paisley dragons' – a sure sign that the band's supplier of their beloved hallucinogens was a reliable one. 'Baby Appeal' was standard, lurching Eighties soul-funk inspired in part by the stripped-down beats of early Grandmaster Flash-led rap and woefully bereft of anything approaching the energy and aggression of the band's punk rock roots; although in bragging of sexual conquests, the quartet laid their cards on the table: they liked sex. 'Buckle Down' is more white boy funk, Jack Sherman's guitars disappointingly low in the mix save for the burst of an electrified solo. This was true of much of the album – the obsession with funk meant that Flea's bass was always in the listener's face, occasionally to the detriment of the six string and the record's melodies.

'Get Up And Jump' was a call to do just that, a frantically fast funk work-out straight from the Prince school, a definite sign of things to come (although the addition of synthesizer horns weakens things somewhat). Lyrically, it was nonsense, littered with made-up words and corny rhymes.

'Why Don't You Love Me' was a catchy cover of Hank Williams' country standard and offered a further glimpse at Kiedis' unique rapping/ talking style that would be used to better effect on later hits. 'Green Heaven' was a classier song and a break from the usual nonsensical sexual boasts. Indeed, it saw the band embarking on a rare political commentary of Los Angeles – and by extension, America – as they saw it, referencing everything from the Ku Klux Klan, author and Church Of Scientology founder L. Ron Hubbard, "trigger happy cops", heroin and prostitutes before ending with a scathing lambast against American tradition. Flea later remembered how excited he was when Anthony presented him with the lyrics to the song and would regularly phone up friends to enthusiastically chant them down the line like a proud father.

'Mommy Where's Daddy' was a pleasant, jazzy jam with some fine saxophone yet that was offset by an uneasy depiction of a father/daughter relationship. 'Out In LA' was the Red Hot Chilli Peppers' first true homage to their home turf and the first to introduce our narrator and Kiedis' aforementioned cheeky alter-ego 'Antwan The Swan' – in the song, Antwan claimed to have got it on with ninety-nine women before being disturbed just as he was about to claim a century score.

Although only one minute long, 'Police Helicopter' was a contender for best song on the album, the one which perhaps came closest to replicating the tight, economical funk-punk of San Pedro three-piece Minutemen, such a big influence on the young Chili Peppers. Even shorter at thirteen seconds long, 'You Always Sing The Same' was a short sharp burst of energy with decidedly minimalist lyrics (basically the title sung a few times), a pastiche of hardcore's penchant for stripping down songs until there was barely anything left. Instrumental album closer 'Grand Pappy Du Plenty' was atmospheric, malevolent and suitably cinematic (hey, this was Hollywood) – as *Kerrang!* rightly described it, "like the music to any early Kurt Russell film, specifically when things 'get personal'." The title was inspired by eccentrically-named Tomato Duplenty, underground artist and one-time frontman with seminal LA band the Screamers, whose popularity and mythical status on the scene in the late Seventies was sealed when they split before ever releasing a record or indeed touring.

The album's cover artwork – an acid-fried gonzo illustration of a bug-eyed band rocking out – was done by comic illustrator Gary Panter, whose *Jimbo* comics were popular amongst LA punk rockers. Any musical and production shortcomings within (and there were many) were over-ridden by a slight suggestion that here was a group who at least promised/aspired to a distinct sound, a unique outlook. Clearly this was a band of brothers (well, two at least), even if they hadn't yet written any stone cold classics. As a whole work, *Red Hot Chili Peppers* was predominantly a record about the City Of Angels and its many flavours – from coyotes running wild in the Hollywood hills to the overhead buzz and searching spotlights of police helicopters; from days spent wandering the sun-baked streets and breathing in the smog to long hot nights of sweaty sexual liaisons. Had the Chili Peppers not gone on to far greater things, it's likely that this inauspicious yet mildly intriguing debut would have disappeared into the bargain bin of musical history. Even the most generous of ears struggles to deny it sounds dated and a little forced. Which, for the increasingly large numbers of people who had been wowed by the band's astonishing live shows, was deeply disappointing.

But it was a signifier of things to come, a calling card from young goofy men out to get laid and have a good time *all the time*. The deep-fried funk had been embraced, and all the key Chili Peppers subjects – LA, sex, partying, the band as a tight-knit brotherhood – had been broached. The party had started.

In later years, commentators would say this laid the very foundation stone for funk metal, that the influences of Parliament/Sly and the Family Stone versus Black Flag/Minutemen/The Germs created an erratic but brave debut that was a watershed moment in rock history. It wasn't. The influences were there, of course, but the album just didn't really work, and the band felt that as much as anyone. They didn't need any critics to tell them that they needed to do better. Flea said so himself. "Our natural, spontaneous thing wasn't there," Flea complained. "If we'd had that original line-up on the first record, I think we would have been a lot more popular a lot sooner. We would have gotten the real thing, hard-core, down on record. We were so explosive at that time - and it's not an explosive record."

At the same time, the two founding members of the Chilis were at pains to point out that they did not hold either Jack Sherman or Cliff Martinez responsible for the problems on the record. As Anthony explained to *LA Weekly*'s John Albert: "Cliff is the coolest drummer of all time, but his shit only spoke to a kind of more refined, intellectual art/funk vision of the world. We loved the hell out of his shit."

Reviews of the album were sparse and, when they surfaced, were muted; sales were worse. Undaunted, the Chili Peppers headed out on their first ever US headline tour in October 1983. During this period, although sales of the album were sluggish, their live following blossomed, particularly in the influential college radio market. Lindy Goetz was working flat out to get them gigs and every time he called them to ask if they could make a show, he always got an immediate 'yes'. These were hard years for the Chilis – on low income from poor record sales, touring much of the USA (predominantly on the west coat and Midwest) in the proverbial rusty van, sleeping in low cost motels and playing to hundreds of people every night in a different town – some enthusiastic, some indifferent. In such an intimate environment, the camaraderie of a band is the lifeblood of their daily survival, but unfortunately as the tour progressed, it became clear that there was a void between Jack Sherman and Flea/Anthony. The latter pair were pure party animals, out on the town every night, sampling the high and low lights of what life on the road had to offer. Sherman tended to stay in most nights. The chemistry could never evolve with such a personality chasm between them. By January, 1984 Sherman was asked to leave the band. Immediately, Flea and Anthony set about courting their former charge Hillel Slovak. Sherman's playing had helped shape the band sound so far and in stepping in to fill Hillel's shoes, he had probably secured the band's very existence – even making the possibility of a debut album a reality. However, when it came down to it, Flea and Anthony wanted their guitar soulmate back. It was a question of deep-rooted loyalty – as far as they saw it, Hillel was their *brother*.

Their timing was perfect as What Is This? had failed to capitalise on a strong start and were on the verge of disintegrating. By the time of Sherman's departure from the Chilis, Hillel's band was effectively over. Despite having previously been busy recording with What Is This?, Hillel had started making regular call to his former bandmates expressing a readiness to return to the fold for some good times, Chili Peppers-style. After some deliberation, Hillel eventually agreed to rejoin the Red Hot Chili Peppers. Jack Irons, despite the demise of What Is This? remained outside the band.

The extent of the Chili Peppers' partying at this stage should not be ignored. They were working very hard but partying equally so. Drugs, inevitably for many bands, played a part in that. Flea admits to having dabbled in many drugs, but it was the future use of heroin by Anthony and Hillel which would escalate into tragedy.

CHAPTER 4

If James Brown is the Godfather of Soul, then George Clinton is the Grandaddy of Funk. The man behind such funk legends as Parliament, Funkadelic and the P-Funk All Stars, Clinton is the human embodiment of what funk is all about. Born some time between 1940 and 1947 (no one seems certain), Clinton was the first of nine children born to a Kannapolis family. He worked initially as a hairdresser at the Newark Uptown Tonsorial Parlor, singing at local hops and even on street corners by night. The ever-changing line-up of his first major act, the Parliaments, did not stop that band becoming one of the true pioneers of funk with records such as 'I Wanna Testify' – ironically, this song was a Top 20 hit in the USA a year after a disillusioned Clinton had abandoned the record business and returned to barber shop work full-time. The mid-to-late 'sixties wave of psychedelic rock (largely a white boy, acid-born phenomenon until the tsunami that was Jimi Hendrix entered the fray) seemed an appropriate groove to cross over into, and Funkadelic was the result.

This was only the beginning of a finely-spun web of funk bands and George Clinton was the spider at its centre. Utilising astonishing musicians, outlandish costumes and a kind of biblical zeal, Clinton made an all-out attack on understatement that brought some considerable success. In 1978 he had a huge hit with 'One Nation Under A Groove', which was supported by a stadium tour around the USA. The Eighties, however, brought legal and financial wrangles that forced him into a lengthy hiatus. Clinton has since proved to be one of the most sampled artists in history. He is a great eccentric, a genuine pioneer and an actual living legend. And any man who can release a record called *You Shouldn't Nuf Bit, Fish!* has to go down in history.

Of course, the Chilis knew all this and simply worshipped Clinton. To meet him was a highlight, to be able to put forward as the man to produce their next album unthinkable. For the so-called Dr Funkenstein to say yes was mere fantasy. But that's what happened.

The paths of funk and rock had crossed way before the Red Hot Chili Peppers began cross-pollinating two differing – but equally hedonistic and colourful – genres. Funk's roots lay in soul and R&B sounds which by the late Sixties began to be influenced by the purple haze that had been drawn over rock music – Jim Hendrix's outlandish style was to be a far-reaching influence. Drugs fuelled creativity and as result minds and musical boundaries began to expand at the dawn of the Seventies. Funk music could soundtrack parties and revolution alike, the domain of both colourful burgeoning exponents like Sly Stone and George Clinton and hardline politicised pro- black separatist factions like the Black Panthers.

With the emergence of landmark releases from artists such as James Brown, Sly & The Family Stone and Stevie Wonder, funk flourished throughout the decade. Funk was raw, primal and deep, and often centred around extended jams and syncopated, highly danceable rhythms. Early funk bands tended to appeal to more hardcore R&B/soul fans but as the genre diversified so its popularity grew, its fanbase and musicians largely black. The music was all about the groove – a factor certainly heavily influenced by James Brown's hit singles like 'Papa Got A Brand New Bag' and epoch-making 'Get Up (I Feel Like Being A) Sex Machine.', both of which would also be provide staple samples to much of early rap and hip-hop. George Clinton had followed in Brown's wake, adding his own colourful style and madcap concepts to funk. Clinton's music was all about excess – in lifestyle, in clothes, in sounds – something which funk shared with the best rock and roll bands: a realisation that this was meant to be *fun* (and it sounds like an exact template for the early Chilis).

So it seemed only natural that the Chilis and George Clinton would cross paths at some point. Indeed, you could argue that had Flea been born in another generation, he would probably have been playing bass for Clinton at some point anyway. Certainly, analogies with Flea could be drawn with former James Brown and then Funkadelic bassist, Bootsy Collins. He joined Clinton in the Seventies and his wild appearance – part-spaceman, part-wizard, part-shaman – made him an instant hit with fans. In addition, his fabulous bass style deepened the tenor of soul music, dragging it into the funk age and separating that band from their peers – surely something which could equally be attributed to Flea.

Although the Chili's work would go on to define – along with material by other bands such as Faith No More and Fishbone – the new sound of 'funk-rock', for now the history books tell us that Clinton was the undisputed heavyweight master of the funk.

The making of the Chili's second album, to be called *Freaky Styley*, was pretty much a party from beginning to end. Buoyed by the recent return of their closest friend, Hillel, Anthony and Flea were incredibly excited about the new record.

To get things rolling before the new sessions, Anthony, Flea and Cliff had enjoyed a break in Mexico where, armed with a four-track and a bag of weed, they wrote the first songs for their sophomore album. The rest of the time was spent riding around on mopeds and eating fine Mexican food.

On their return to Hollywood, it was confirmed that the band had pulled off their biggest coup to date: George Clinton had indeed agreed to produce the record. The band was elated that one of their heroes, the godfather of funk, wanted to be involved. Flea and manager Lindy flew out to meet Dr Funkenstein in Detroit, where they were given a warm welcome by Clinton and his P-funk crew. The band followed suit, setting up home at a condo on a golf course in Bloomfield Hills, one of Detroit's more affluent areas.

For Flea, this was one moment which he later said was a memory he would always cherish: "Meeting George Clinton, I was so nervous because he is Dr Funkenstein, this other worldly mythological character and I walked into this motel room and there he was, just the warmest, kindest, most beautiful person I've ever met in my life. That moment I will never forget."

It had been perhaps surprising that rather than working in the heat and madness of LA, Clinton invited the band to his country retreat studio outside Detroit. For a funk legend and a funk-rock band, this seemed somewhat incongruous – after all, the Motor City was more famed for the MC5, the Stooges and all things garage punk. However, this quieter environment seemed to work as the Chili Peppers quickly wrote thirteen brand new songs.

This wasn't to say that they had lost their famed energy – although they found that Clinton in person was much more subdued and mellow than the larger-then-life caricature that was presented to the public, the Chili Peppers themselves wasted no time rooting out all the best experiences that Detroit nightlife had to offer.

Studio time was also very relaxed – whereas the first album had been rigidly formulated using click tracks for example, this time Clinton would dance around the studio, clapping and clicking his fingers and shouting, "Yeah, kick it, throw it down!" every ten seconds. This naturally dovetailed perfectly with the Chili Peppers' own spontaneity and vibrancy and made the whole recording experience much more enjoyable than that on *Red Hot Chili Peppers*.

Their was no shortage of narcotic usage for the band during the making of *Freaky Styley,* including coke – some say the funk musician's drug of choice – and the Chilis were making the most of it, partying all day and into the night before heading back to their condo "to crash as best we could."

To make the sessions even more enticing, Clinton invited various acolytes from his revered musician circles to play with the Chilis in the studio – luminaries such as Maceo Parker and Fred Wesley, associates of his and famed for their work in the Seventies with James Brown. Surrounded by such talent, it was inevitable that the Chilis produced a much stronger record than their debut effort, and perhaps not surprising given Clinton's notorious semantic acrobatics that the album came with the enigmatic title, *Freaky Styley*.

Considering the many funk rock albums that were to appear over the next half decade or so, *Freaky Styley* has weathered reasonably well. With a genuine connoisseur of the funk sound at the controls, the album was packed full of the deep grooves the band had been striving for and saw them step up a level in the playing to achieve a sense of consistency throughout. But once again it was let down by an absence of what certain cynically-minded types at major record labels would term, 'hits'. As Flea proudly put it, more than any other record the Chilis would make, this album falls into the category of "too funky for white radio, too punk rockin' for black." The standard pop format was nowhere to be seen.

As with their debut, *Freaky Styley* began with some booming rock in the shape of the twitching 'Jungleman'. Prodigal son Hillel's post-punk guitars and the old trick of band singalong choruses made for a potent album opening, exactly what you would expect from four white funk fans let loose with their spiritual mentor. Steeped in Seventies funk flavour and some neatly arranged horns (courtesy of 'The Horny Horns', no less) 'Hollywood (Africa)' was a well-executed and complimentary cover version of New Orleans funk legends The Meters' 'Africa', one of the catchiest moments on the album and later re-titled when the band transplanted the essence of the song to more familiar neighbourhood. It's a song Bootsy Collins would have been proud of. 'American Ghost Dance' was more low down and dirty funk. Concerned with the white man's pillaging of Indian land, an atrocity that twisted the heart of modern America, it's about as political as the Chili Peppers get. And while it may bear the hallmarks of a young band gingerly dabbling in politics, the Chilis at least felt moved enough to comment where previously they had only largely been concerned with singing about pussy. And tits.

Both 'Nevermind' and their cover of Sly Stone's 'If You Want Me To Stay' were album highlights, two songs that would linger in the Chilis' canon as future B-side or live favourites, while most of the other *Freaky Styley* tracks would be forgotten about as the band moved onto bigger and better things. Starting with some fine lyrical self-aggrandisement from Anthony, 'Nevermind' was a band signature tune, a song whose predominant aim was to announce the arrival of "The Red Hot...Chili... Peppers!" with suitable aplomb over a slap-bass backbeat. Clearly the band had not only been influenced by the sound of funk, but the presentation too. After all, Clinton was the king of grand gestures and self-referencing lyrics tunes – the king of entertainment in the Seventies, more colourful even than Elvis.

The album's more-or-less instrumental title track was something of an interlude in amongst all those driving funk rhythms - the drags on a cigarette after half an album's worth of musical rutting. The short interlude was something the band would return to again and again. 'Blackeyed Blonde' was a chance for Flea to put his nimble-fingered dexterity in practice. Despite the jaw-dropping speed funk that drove it and Slovak's 'Superfly'-style wah-wah guitar it was less a song and more a precision jam, although it was also notable for having vocal breaks where the band made like chimps – and sounded great!

'The Brothers Cup' was a Flea and Anthony friendship song. They were often to be seen wearing leather jackets with cups hooked onto the shoulder (you can see an illustration of Anthony in full brothers cup mode on a later re-issue of the album). What it meant no-one quite knew – maybe a sign of their poverty, a suggestion they were one step away from pan-handling with their portable cups if necessary? Flea even accompanied Clinton to an Aretha Franklin show in Detroit wearing his cups.

'Battleship' was notable for being a slice of the punk-reared Chili Peppers thrash of their early live shows, but this was a funk album so the song just seemed out of place by comparison. 'Lovin' And Touchin' ' wasn't a highlight either, not least because the idea of the Red Hot Chili

Peppers being all caring, earnest and sensual was at complete odds with their locker room depictions of sex. Thankfully it was very short. The contentiously-titled 'Catholic School Girls Rule' was an instantaneously infectious harder-edged tune that had as much to do with the boasts of hip-hop – proof that in their readiness to musically cross-pollinate styles and ideas the Chili Peppers were way ahead of rap/metal crossover bands like Limp Bizkit and Korn who would emerge in the mid-Nineties. The Chilis were chopping and changing, rhyming and stealing way before it was fashionable for a rock band to do so.

Unfortunately, by the time the album reached 'Sex Rap', it was beginning to feel like *Freaky Styley* was running very thin on ideas and Kiedis' attempts at rapping were beginning to lose their charm. 'Thirty Dirty Birds' was a dumb twelve second poem – actually more a cluster of rhyming lines than a poetic work – delivered by Anthony in a pastiche *New Yoik* accent. 'Yertle The Turtle' was one last funk freakout, fun-packed with a horn section to get people on the dancefloor. And, yes, it really was a rather strange little allegorical story about a turtle called Yertle. Well, why not? The sleeve for the album was a collage of shots of the band leaping and gurning through the air against a Renaissance-era painting, a cover as daft and colourful as the music within. At the same time, these photos seemed a little like they were lagging behind the band's evolution, an image and presentation that was still stuck in their teens.

Despite its more politicised moments, this was still a blatantly lustful album which clearly reinforced the connection between funk and sex. The band's enjoyment of, and interest in sex was lavished all over the project. Fortunately, it didn't ruin the record. With the warmth and mutual respect between the band and Clinton, the whole experience was enjoyed by everybody involved, a pleasing contrast to the problems of the first album. Flea went on to say that Clinton was "an epic, mythological genius."

At the time, the critics were unsure and the public were only mildly impressed. Furthermore, this was a record of extremes, fusing hardcore and dance, funk and punk, so it was probably not surprising that it would struggle to enjoy mainstream radio support – something which Flea's earlier comments about black and white radio had predicted.

Sales were again modest, although those who did own the album revelled in it and fuelled word of mouth on the band. They still had no record deal in the UK and only a small handful of European territories had the record in miniscule quantities on import. This was hardly an album to change the world, brave as it was.

Opinions on *Freaky Styley* still remain divided to this day. Many class it as the odd-one-out for the Chilis, the 'freaky' album that doesn't quite fit into their catalogue. The more rock-minded of their fans largely don't even own it. Yet in many ways it is the typical Chilis record. Okay, their instrumentation and above all *songwriting* would improve vastly in records to come, but the very heart of this record was all about funk, and that is where the essence of the Chili Peppers emanates from.

Okay, it bears little resemblance to the band who would score huge hits with songs like 'Scar Tissue' and 'Zephyr Song', yet in making an album of hard funk party songs, the band had realised a dream, achieved what they had wanted to achieve with their second album. Few people could argue *Freaky Styley* is the Chili Peppers' finest work to date, but it was an essential part in the evolution of the band, a leap forward musically and, the end of an era later described by Flea as "giving me very powerful feelings of elation and melancholy with the memories of Hillel swimming all around…"

This very particular record also presented the Chilis with something of a dilemma. Already seen by some as pioneers, their commercial success was nevertheless still rather muted. At the same time, the album's detractors suggested that the band's single biggest asset – their live show – was not really visible on the vinyl. On stage the Chilis were so *physical*, yet with Clinton never having seen one of their gigs, this did not really translate to the record itself. And in many ways, without this physicality, the Chilis lost their uniqueness. Oddly, the mixing engineer performed the final mix down without Clinton, which seemed to be an unusual step to some, but that was not the root of the problem. The Chilis, despite this worthy effort, were still not in full flow. They were the Jekyll and Hide of the alternative scene – one night you might see them live and pronounce them to be the greatest band that has ever existed; the next you might listen to either of their first two albums and turn the volume down – or even off.

At least the Chilis had a big tour lined up to remind people of exactly what they were best at. Although the crowds at their shows still remained predominantly frat boys and college music buffs, there were signs that *Freaky Styley* had broadened that demograph somewhat. Despite the set list containing an unduly large number of sexual songs, this tour saw more women in the audience as well as some inkling of an older audience too.

Apart from the obvious US dates, the Chilis played their first overseas show on this tour, when they performed at a German festival, later to be joined by George Clinton on a TV show before flying to the UK for their debut show there. At first, the British Isles were not particularly warm to the Chilis, beginning a love/hate relationship with the UK that at first was very much 'hate'. The irony that this was a raging live band represented on disc as something quite different did not help their international cause. They remained a band without profile outside of their established, growing but fairly cultish home audience.

It was perhaps small wonder that the UK was not too enamoured with the peculiarly LA sound of the Chili Peppers. The 1980s are often remembered as a dull period for UK pop and rock music, or – if not dull – then at least unadventurous. The Red Hot Chili Peppers had launched their career at a time when post-punk and new wave bands drifted into a kind of watered-down glam, the excitement of the original era of Bowie, Bolan and Roxy Music in the UK and The New York Dolls in the States filtered down to the likes of Culture Club, Duran Duran and Adam & The Ants, pale though entertaining shadows of their forebears. Rock, with a capital 'R' drifted back to the mainstream, and although the likes of John Lydon and The Clash soldiered on, it was the camp cock-rock of Guns N' Roses, the anodyne background music of Dire Straits and the ubiquitous Bruce Springsteen who gave the impression that punk had never happened.

The Eighties weren't all about Kylie Minogue and Jason Donovan however (no more than, say, the Seventies were all about The Bay City Rollers and David Cassidy). Bands such as The Smiths in the UK and REM in America proved that there were articulate, sensitive and highly amusing furrows for rock to plough. Small wonder though, with Morrissey talking of gritty urban Mancunian vistas and teen bubblegum pop dominating the TV screens, that a bunch of seemingly nihilistic, sexually-charged LA funksters was not everyone's, er, cup of tea.

Back on the road with the Chilis, despite most of these live shows being rapturously received, the chemistry was still not perfect and on the band's return to the US, Cliff Martinez went his separate ways from the other three. In his stool came... Jack Irons. The rotating personnel of the Red Hot Chili peppers had finally come full circle to the original line-up. Immediately, the difference was apparent – rave reviews for their live shows flooded in and it was clear that Hillel and Jack had made a pivotal difference to the make-up of the Chilis. Suitably fired up, the band headed off for a mammoth tour in the winter of 1985, including shows with Run DMC, which pretty much covered most of America.

But this was not all about the music. If only it were that simple. Never ones to shy away from the licence to party that comes with being in a touring band, the Chili Peppers were starting to crumble. The candle was being burnt at both ends. This was, after all, a band whose unofficial motto was borrowed from Captain Beefheart: "Hit it to hell in the breadbasket and fingerfuck the devil." Not a signal that they were about to slow down. Something – or someone – might get hurt.

Their touring schedule was hectic, no one would deny that, but that is what the Chilis loved. The more gigs the better. They personally chose to use a variety of drugs, recreationally, to ease the pressures from time to time and, often, just to have a good time. Jack was largely indifferent to the drug lifestyle, Flea made no secret that he experimented but he was beginning to get bored, but Anthony and Hillel were something altogether different. Both Slovak and Kiedis began to wage an equally riotous campaign to reduce the nation's drug stocks and to ingest as much as they could. They took the drugs. They took heroin. Anthony didn't deny it; Hillel did. Despite Irons' and Flea's protestations the pair developed a lifestyle destined to end in tragedy.

Anthony later talked very openly about this problem on VH-1's *Behind The Music* special on the band: "It really kind of ended up sinking its teeth into me over the course of a coupla years. I would do it one weekend and I would go to band practice every day and I would say, I won't do that for a coupla weeks, then I won't do that for a week and then I won't do that or a few days. Then (I'd say) well I did just do it yesterday but this will be the only time that I do it two days in a row… I just sort of starting buying the lie."

He went on to say, " Hillel started a little bit later than I did and was equally naïve that our life was being sucked away. We were just too swallowed up to be cognisant of it and say, 'Whoah! We gotta stop this.' At that point, you are gone."

The problem was that where before they had enjoyed their own 'brotherhood', a closely-knit gaggle of musicians with so much in common, the drug use was starting to polarise the Chilis into two camps. Flea later said that, "I wish I could have been there for (Hillel) more.

And with Anthony, when I see him go thru his troubles, I love Anthony, I want to be there with him." Hillel's playing on stage each night became increasingly erratic; his studio work didn't seem to suffer but his body and health certainly seemed to. Anthony tried to face some of his demons head on. Hillel denied he was using. Slovak began to turn his back on the support of his friends and pushed his increasing habit underground. While Flea married girlfriend Loesha Zeivar in 1985 – having her name lovingly tattooed around his nipple – Slovak became more and more of a problem within the band itself. The problem escalated. The tour through winter 1985 was a largely scrappy, unimpressive affair and it was not a good omen for the future.

CHAPTER 5

With barely a pause for breath after returning from their mammoth tour, the Chilis began to formulate their next album, their third in as many years. The band reconvened in the studio in January 1987 to begin work on the new project. It is ironic that by the time the Chili Peppers came to make the album they'd always wanted to, the record that would help spread the good word of the funky monks around the globe, they were at an all-time low. Drug-use was rife – no change there then – yet for the first time was beginning to impinge on attitudes within the band and effect communication. Nevertheless the quartet held it together at a pivotal time and came up with an album that rightly should have heralded the breakthrough they had been waiting for.

After an aborted demo session with one-time Clash guitarist Keith Levene, then playing with John Lydon's Public Image Limited (plus a rumoured decision not to work with Malcolm McLaren), the band hooked up with producer Michael Beinhorn at Los Angeles' Capitol Studios. – who had made sizzling records with Herbie Hancock and Nona Hendryx and went onto work with Marilyn Manson, Korn and Aerosmith - and entered Capitol Studios on Vine in Hollywood. Beinhorn has appeared as producer and keyboard player on a number of albums, including Korn's *Untouchables* and *Here To Stay*, as well as Ozzy Osbourne's *Ozmosis*. With a record collection of his own that included Fela Kuti, Stevie Wonder, Jimi Hendrix and Sly Stone, he was clearly coming to the party from a similar zone as the Chilis' own. Technically, he was also a producer of great wisdom – he helped develop the Ultra Analog recording format that brings out low-end bass sound – ideal for bigging up Flea's sound in the studio. The Chili Peppers – balanced as they were on the brink of major label success and on the edge of a descent into drug-fuelled self-destruction – were perhaps in the safest hands of all in terms of keeping their career on track.

"I recall it as a gloomy time in our career," noted Flea in the sleeve-notes to the 2003 re-release of the album. "Drug use was really beginning to make a morose stand." Record mogul Rick Rubin visited the band in the studios at this time and he later told them that walking in to see them one day had been "the most depressing-feeling rooms he had ever been in." By their own admission, the band and their world at this time were "ugly".

Luckily for them, Beinhorn refused to let a far-from-promising start spoil the sessions – they'd shown up to record the album with only five songs completed, so he duly lambasted them and ordered them to go and bring back more, chastising them for their laziness in the process. This was to be a far stricter regime than that of George Clinton. His pursuit of the band's very best even went so far as to see him join them on tour to capture their true essence. Correctly realising that they were essentially a *live* band, Beinhorn set about capturing the breath-taking energy of a Chili Peppers show on record.

Opening the album with the band's finest moment to date, the slamming 'Fight Like A Brave', was a wise move - a sign that even if this was a band on the brink of destruction, with both Slovak and Irons back in place they were playing better than ever. Their two previous albums might have seen the Chilis trying to marry their twin loves of punk rock and funk, but 'Fight Like A Brave' was the first that achieved it successfully and was soon to become a keystone song in the burgeoning funk metal scene over the coming three years or so. Just to hammer the point home, 'Funky Crime' followed. With the hook line *"Funk is my attitude"* and Hillel Slovak's guitar-riffs-from-the-groin the band made it clear what they were all about, though it's anyone's guess what a 'funky crime' might entail. A Funkadelic-fused tale of brotherly love that was something of a running theme throughout the album, 'Me & My Friends' is fittingly still a live staple song to this day – the oldest in the set.

'Backwoods' was later said to be partly inspired by a recent meeting with for Sex Pistols manager Malcolm McLaren. The red-haired svengali had expressed interest in producing the Red Hot Chili Peppers' third album and had arranged to meet with them in the parking lot of EMI. When a Rolls Royce pulled up and a figure stepped out in "adorned in flowing white robes and majestically strolled up, soiling the bottoms of his shoes in our parking" the band were impressed. McLaren then went onto to detail his plans for the band: they would play basic Chuck Berry-inspired rock and roll while dressed in the latest skate punk clothes and Anthony would be the star of the band. The relationship between the quartet and the English fop went no further, although they were inspired enough by his talk to write a song that saw a return to the roots of rock, the driving, funk-fest of 'Backwoods', which namechecks the likes of Chuck Berry and Howlin' Wolf. So maybe McLaren was not so far off the mark after all…

RED HOT CHILI PEPPERS

The raucous breakbeat punk-funk pile-up 'Skinny Sweaty Man' was written in homage to the band's own guitarist after a memorable band night out during the making of previous album *Freaky Styley*. They'd been out *en masse* to see some bands and get wasted and in a moment of fuelled inspiration had seized one of the band's equipment before they could return for an encore. Wearing a sharp green suit, Slovak had stormed the dance floor "like a crazy freak." A new nickname – and a new song – was born.

'Behind The Sun' was a cod-psychedelic song that, lyrically at least, could have been written by a quasi-spiritual Venice Beach surf rat burn-out, being as it is about talking dolphins and "the pulse beat of the earth". With sitars and Flea's warm thumping bass it was, song words aside, something of an understated Chilis classic – an attempt to do something different which worked beautifully.

An energised hard funk cover of Bob Dylan's 'Subterranean Homesick Blues' – one of rock's most holy shrines and a difficult act to pull off – may have disgruntled a few acid casualties and old folkies but, as with all good cover versions, the Chilis somehow managed to reinvent the song as their own. Kiedis' barking rap style was also fully unveiled in a time when the worlds of rock and rap had still not quite converged in modern music. Anyone unaware of Dylan's work could certainly have been convinced it was a recent Chili's composition – surely a compliment of the highest order.

If 'Skinny Sweaty Man' was the Chilis at their daftest, then 'Party On Your Pussy' – called 'Special Secret Song Inside' on the album at the behest of a worried EMI - saw them at their dumbest. Suitably slinky and annoyingly addictive it boasted of yet more sexual conquests and antics. To the Chilis'growing band of frowning critics, it did little to dispel the notion that the Red Hot Chili Peppers were anything more than just sexist jocks. The LA scene in 1987 was awash with glam rock Neanderthals like Motley Crue boasting of other such sexual conquests so such pointless idiocy was neither new nor indeed particularly out of the ordinary and 'Special Secret Song Inside' certainly wasn't one of their finer moments.

'No Chump Love Sucker' was the album's hardest moment, pure funk-metal that the likes of Living Colour, Fishbone and Faith No More were beginning to ply around the same time. A bilious take on a sexual encounter gone bad, it rocked from beginning to end. 'Walking On Down The Road' was another slap-bass led song, mid-paced but suitably anthemic. Full of cringeworthy sexual metaphors and innuendo – Kiedis' lyrical style wasn't getting any stronger - 'Love Trilogy' was let down by no-brain lyrics that to some seemed crass in a time when the world was gripped by an AIDS crisis. Not vindictive of course, but badly-thought out perhaps? A joke without a punch-line. Musically, it made up for any shortcomings, with Flea's arpeggios on his bass speeding up to ahardcore-like climax.

'Organic Anti-Beat Box Band' book-ended the album with opener 'Fight Like A Brave' nicely. Another long-term future live favourite, it was all the many flavours of the album distilled down into one funk jam that spawned the title of the record, a colourful squall of noise complete with wah-wah guitars and a tribal sing-a-long chorus. Subject-wise it was sex music all the way – from the suggestive to the hilarious to the crude: Kiedis had made no bones about what his favourite past time was.

As the band themselves would later admit, the album's only really stylistic weakness was to over-utilize triggered drums sounds, a now-dated sounding technique that smoothes out the primal human rhythms that are at the heart of rock and roll music.

Wrapped up in a suitably colourful sleeve that suggested a party was going on inside, the record was (rather fantastically) called *The Uplift Mofo Party Plan*. It was an album that saw all the musicians excelling in ability – whether that was Flea pioneering his slap-bass sound, Slovak's fluid style or Irons' ability to lock down a beat so distinctly – all four members coalescing into a cohesive and refreshing sound which, was for the first time, resolutely the Red Hot Chilli Peppers.

Uplift... is probably the rockingest [sic] record we ever made," noted Flea in the sleeve-notes to a 2003 re-release of the album. "I don't mean the best, though to some it might be, I just mean in terms of straight-up rockin' and not giving a fuck, making some art. This record really brings the rock funk and art in just the way we wanted it to at the time. We were crazy as shit and on a highway to hell, but we did it, we pulled it off."

Regardless of the worrying atmosphere surrounding this album, the commercial impact was impressive. Within two months of its release, *The Uplift Mofo Party Plan* had sold more than the band's first two albums *put together*. In so doing, it had finally ended the major label underachievers tag that some unkind observers had labelled them with since they had signed to EMI for eight albums. What is more, the reviews were starting to talk about the band as "influential", "pioneering" and so on. The Chilis – professionally at least – seemed to have turned the corner.

And yet, The Chili Peppers were fairly at odds with the general flavour of top-selling pop for the time: Michael Jackson's *Thriller* and Bruce Springsteen's *Born In The USA*, released the previous year, were competing as the albums that everyone had to own. Springsteen's bleak portrayal of a post-Vietnam America dressed up in fist-punching optimism was misunderstood by the majority of Americans, who interpreted its tone as pure Reagan-ite jingoism. Fist punching a-plenty was also visible at the two Live Aid concerts held in London and at the JFK Stadium in Philadelphia, where Queen, David Bowie, Sting, U2, The Who, Led Zeppelin and a plethora of other rock icons shook the conscience of the world with their call for aid to Africa.

The conservatism of the Reagan/Thatcher years had also brought with it a call for "more responsible art", whatever that is, with censor groups enjoying new popularity. The year closed with Tipper Gore – the self-acclaimed social conscience of the nation and wife of Senator Al Gore – urging record companies and retailers to label products accordingly if they contained lyrics or material of a dubious or immoral nature. Frank Zappa labelled the demands of Gore's Parents' Music Resources Center "some sinister kind of toilet training," but the voices of dissent were not only those of left-fielders like Zappa. Criticism of the scheme came also from the mild-mannered darling of bespectacled folk-country, John Denver. This all seemed a long way away from what the Chili Peppers were doing – after all, they had songs such as 'Party On Your Pussy' on general release. The zeitgeist of the time, at least in the mainstream seemed against them – but despite this, or maybe because of it, people still went out and bought the album.

However, some argued that this prevailing cultural environment was *exactly* what the Chilis needed to start to penetrate the mainstream. Funk is defined by its hard-hitting, pulsating bass lines and sexual, primal rhythms. At a time when the ethos of Gordon Gekko was more popular than that of Mother Theresa, it was perhaps a fitting time for funk to be reborn. Fuelled through the Seventies by easily available drugs and equally available sex, 'funk' bands like Sly & The Family Stone, Parliament and Funkadelic were enjoying renewed success and critical acclaim. Time for their natural protégés to come to the fore perhaps?

In contrast to the commercial progress made with the healthy sales of *Mofo Party Plan*, initial responses from the critics frustrated the band. Although rap had been a part of their make-up for five years already, the initial single release 'Fight Like A Brave' was compared to the newly emergent Beastie Boys, and some critics even suggested the Chili Peppers were copying these new punks on the block. There was always a rivalry of some kind between the two bands. Even though their music was different there did seem to be an East Coast/West Coast rivalry friction going on there. Perhaps worse, it was suggested that the Peppers had done to funk what some accused The Beastie Boys of doing to rap – sanitizing it for a white audience and increasing the marginalisation of the original black musicians who created the format in the first place. There was nothing new in this: regardless of their individual merits, white singers and bands have always appropriated black music and claimed the lion's share of the audience, income and profile for their own. No less a band than The Beatles had lifted liberally from Motown in their early years, while a decade later the frantic energy of the early Jackson Five was made palatable for middle-class white America by The Osmond Brothers' act. But surely this seemed an unfairly harsh critique of the Chili Peppers? More reasonable perhaps to state that the Chili Peppers would raise the profile of funk for a white audience. This band was clearly *within* the tradition of funk, not commenting upon it from outside.

As ever, it was the fans that gave the band their clearest message. Two years had passed since the last album, and in that time the touring schedule of the band had built up an eager live audience, anticipating the next release. Perhaps tiring of the scandals involving Colonel Oliver North and the arms-for-hostages crisis at The White House, the collapse of the New York stock market and the continued insanity of a world in which a van Gogh painting sold for over $50 million, a section America was ready to party. On the release of the album this live fraternity came out in their droves, and from the small crowds that the Peppers had grown used to they now had no problem drawing over a thousand a night to their gigs, supported by the then relatively little-known Faith No More. Still limited to playing medium-sized halls, at least they could now fill them. Although radio play was not great yet, the gigs were often frenzied nights, with rioters and police colliding as the band's furious live sound provided a theatrical backdrop. Europe too began to come on board – 'Fight Like A Brave,' released as a single in the UK, receiving good notices.

Regardless of their apparent uneasy placement in the social culture and rock/pop lexicon of the time, this third album would ultimately herald the Chili Peppers as genuine pioneers. But as mentioned above, they were not alone. Inevitably, old school funk had found itself indelibly staining other musical genres throughout the Seventies and Eighties – and it is important to highlight that the Chili Peppers were *not* the very first band to fuse it with rock. The first band to successfully mix funk and rock actually remain relatively obscure today. Formed in Atlanta, Mother's Finest were a multi-racial bands that between the years of 1976 and 1983 released a series of records that shattered the genre divides. Rock bands had certainly taken excursions into funk before – most notably Aerosmith on 'Sweet Emotion' and Led Zeppelin's 'The Ocean' – but it still had been within the domain of the relatively orthodox white boy rock set up. Mother's Finest took the blend to another level, mixing up Led Zeppelin's rock and roll heart with the more sinuous, deep throat of Parliament. Yet, Mother's Finest suffered largely for being ahead of their time – too rock for black radio, too funky for the middle American rock crowd.

It was a couple of years into the Chili's career that the seeds of funk–rock – or what was soon to become funk-metal – were sown. The year 1985 had seen the release of that George Clinton-produced album *Freaky Styley* but also debut releases from energetic Hollywood outfit – and long-term friends of the Chili's – Fishbone and 'We Care A Lot' by artsy post-punk/funk San Franciscans Faith No More. The latter's early sound was certainly a strange brew and with the later addition of singer Mike Patton would soon develop into and funk-metal mix to match the Red Hot Chili Peppers, with whom they would soon be rivals of sorts. A motley crew with volatile in-band relationships right from the start, Faith No More were as at odds with the mid-Eighties' cock-rock Sunset Strip scene as the Red Hot Chili Peppers. Between them, both bands would be leaders to a wave of lesser pretenders later in the decade.

The Chili's *The Uplift Mofo Party Plan* was the album that opened the funk-metal floodgates with bands that filled that gap that emerged in the late Eighties between cheesy hair metal and the grunge of the early Nineties. Later, in 1989, Faith No More's groundbreaking album *The Real Thing* was released to great success and critical applause. Where the Chilli Peppers always viewed funk as high-energy party music to soundtrack the good times, Faith No More favoured a darker sound made unique by bassist Bill Gould's funk-inspired bottom-end slap bass sounds and peppered with Roddy Bottum's epic and atmospheric keyboard sounds.

Faith No More's music was equally as powerful and irreverent as the Chilis, but where their LA counterparts celebrated their brotherly bond, the San Franciscans were more belligerent, less overtly wacky. Fresh-faced frontman Mike Patton – who at the age of twenty joined the band straight out of college in time to record *The Real Thing* – was pretty enough for mainstream rock audiences and MTV and eccentric enough to garner the band plenty of press – not least because of his interest in all things scatological. A mere six months after Patton joined the band, they released a lead-off single 'Epic' to great success in January 1990 and found themselves touring with the likes of Guns 'N' Roses and Metallica, both of whom declared them their new favourite band. A rivalry arose between the Chilis and Faith No More – perhaps partly because a large part of Patton's stage persona seemed to directly ape many of Kiedis' moves. When later accused of this, Patton began to mercilessly slag off his counterpart at every available opportunity. Faith No More would later even incorporate a dismissive, Vegas-style version of the 1992 Chili's classic 'Under The Bridge' into their live set.

The ascension of both bands to the upper echelons of the *Billboard* charts ran in tandem. Though their own takes on funk-metal were different in many ways and the emergence of funk-metal more down to coincidence, their respective successes would soon give birth to a new genre. Suddenly bands who had been previously piling on the hairspray and tottering around Sunset in their high heels were reinventing themselves in tie-dye tops, long shorts and fat Nike high top trainers. Funk metal was definitely a case of the few good, the many bad and the largely ugly. As with other rock and metal sub-genres like thrash or speed metal – or even glam rock – funk-metal was resolutely male-orientated music played from the groin rather than the head or the heart and suffered at the hands of critics accordingly.

But aside from its two major protagonists, funk-rock did have a few other notable exponents. As with heavy metal, funk-rock was also an excuse to show off musical prowess and ability. Living Colour were talented musicians and one of the first all-black bands to carve a niche within the hard rock scene of the Eighties, then still dominated by white boys with guitars. The strong influence of rap and hip-hop that exists with rock and metal today had yet to permeate hard rock music, then a far more conservative sound, so it's no overstatement to say this band helped break boundaries. Their 1989 album *Cult* saw off all competitors to win 'Best Hard Rock Album' at that year's Grammy's. Old Chili Peppers cohorts Fishbone were similarly as successful, their entire sound and, in particular their visceral live shows dedicated to maximum energy, combining funk, punk and ska to powerful effect.

Les Claypool's Primus certainly shared some of the same slap-bass sound as their funk-rock but they were just as much influenced by Frank Zappa, post-punk and Rush. They built a lasting career (and famously wrote the theme tune to *South Park*), but only because they were far more inventive and diverse than the identikit funk boys. Their 1999 album *Antipop* featured a plethora of different producers including Rage Against The Machine's Tom Morello, Limp Bizkit's Fred Durst, Tom Waits and even *South Park* creator Matt Stone.

The misleadingly-titled Extreme were serious musos inspired by the pop sensibilities of The Beatles and the flair of Van Halen and Queen who were also given the funk-metal tag early on in their careers, though in reality their sound was at the other end of the musical spectrum from that of the Red Hot Chili Peppers and closer to ropey rock bands like Kings X and Winger. Despite starting out as a funk-based rock band their crossover hit 'More Than Words' was an Everley Brothers-style ballad – Extreme were to last only marginally longer than the genre itself.

All sorts of other miscreants, bandwagoneers and reconstructed guitar heroes emerged in 1990/1991 on the back of funk metal – groups like Mindfunk, King Of The Hill, Ludachrist, Electric Boys – but the genre was effectively over within a couple of years. Even without the emergence of harder, dirtier altogether more believable bands from the Pacific northwest like Nirvana, Mudhoney and Tad – making music that was soon to be called grunge – at a similar time it's doubtful funk-metal would have developed any further.

So between them, the Red Hot Chili Peppers and Faith No More had lit fires in the imaginations of others that burned brightly but briefly. When those flames fizzled out, so too did those bands who were leaders rather than followers, leaving behind a wave of bands now consigned to musical history. What had started out as a vibrant and successful attempt at musical cross-pollination by the Chili Peppers in the early Eighties had developed into something else entirely; something that lacked the colourful humour and punk energy and, most importantly, the devotion to original funk.

Yet, for all it faults, funk metal did inspire other bands that followed in the Nineties. Rage Against The Machine effectively married the hardest funk with metal riffs and hip-hop delivery to spellbinding effect, while other bands like Korn, Incubus and Skunk Anansie all added new angles to straightforward rock and metal by digging in with a deep bass sound to rattle out of speakers the world over. It was far cry from the sounds of Funkadelic and James Brown of course. Perhaps the most successful act of late to mix up the flamboyance of funk with the brute force and showmanship of rock music are Outkast, a duo whose sound straddles genres with extreme confidence and an inherent love of *da fonk*.

Whatever the pros and cons of funk metal, the Red Hot Chili Peppers' part in its history cannot be denied. The problem for the Chilis was, would they follow a path set by many in the funk metal genre and soon be last year's fashion too? Only time would tell. The problem was, the way the Chili Peppers were starting to crumble behind the scenes, there was every chance that they might not make it to next year.

CHAPTER 6

There were rumours that Hillel Slovak was becoming more and more of a liability on the road. Whispers spread quickly of gigs where he played just one song all night long while the rest of the band worked bravely to paper over the cracks through the actual set-list. Terrifying quantities of narcotics seemed to be involved, and both on and off-stage he was becoming more of a problem and a frantic worry to the rest of the band. Distanced from all his contacts on the tour, he became increasingly weak in appearance, haunted and clearly in serious trouble.

As the tour continued so the band courted inadvertent controversy when various groups – notably the Parents Music Resource Center – campaigned against what they called their sexist lyrics and 'obscene' live shows. As mentioned, EMI had already forced them to change the track 'Party On Your Pussy' to 'Special Secret Song,' despite the band's protests, and while the censors sought ever more ridiculous ways of taming this apparent bunch of moral-free hoodlums (a 'Parental Advisory' or 'Warning – Explicit Lyrics' sticker placed on an album sleeve remains one of the best ways of making sure a teenage fan buys an album) it was the power of the music itself that won the day. The band itself made the point that their own behaviour on stage was a separate issue to the nature of their songs on disc, but it's hard to deny that songs like 'Party On Your Pussy,' 'Backwoods' and gigs where socks alone covered the dicks of the otherwise naked band would cause concern among the moral majority. And a band claiming that their music is intended to 'give you an erection' is hardly going to win that particular argument. Nor were tales of how the rest of the band tried to 'inspire' Kiedis while he recorded his tracks for 'Fight Like A Brave' by pressing their bare bollocks against the studio window.

But this fun-loving, hard-rocking, drug-taking bunch of male-bonding sock-wearers hit the heights of the *Billboard* chart at last. Although it doesn't sound exactly historically important in retrospect, the fact that *Uplift Mofo Party Plan* made it to the heady heights of #148 meant that – on the back of all the publicity that the tour and off-stage were getting – there was a growing anticipation for what the band would do next. In the context of the post-Millennial record business, dried up on expense accounts, costly manufactured pop bands and exorbitantly pricey videos, any new act still sitting outside of the Top 100 after this many albums would be cut from the roster as soon as you could say 'You only sold how many?' Had the Chili Peppers been born twenty years later and reached #143 like this, they would never have made another record. Fortunately, back in 1987 the relative 'success' of *Uplift Mofo Party Plan* left people wondering about the band. Musical geniuses? Self-promoting magicians? Fucked-up junkies? Whatever it was going to be, *something* would happen in the Red Hot Chili Peppers camp, and increasingly both their fans and the rock press wanted to be there when it happened.

Sadly, what happened next was only too inevitable, almost a rock cliché, and almost too much to handle for the band itself and still survive. Hillel Slovak died.

It had almost seemed to become more important to party than to rock out. The story is simple and all too common in rock history. The band that works hard, plays hard and gets to the very edge of success, then hits a major crisis as the lifestyle overtakes them. Too often there are casualties, and it is too easy for those casualties (Morrison, Hendrix, Cobain etc) to become lionised, heroes instead of victims, tragic figures who die for no reason. You could argue it could have been others in the Chili Peppers who succumbed first. Anthony was very near the brink too – gradually conceding practical band leadership to Flea as his own addiction worsened. But Slovak cracked on more than one occasion. At the Mean Fiddler in London he simply put his guitar down and walked off stage, his face exhausted, his spirit breaking. It was the first of many such walk-outs, or of nights when his playing was just not up to scratch (and theirs was not your average three chord stomp as the Chilis' catalogue was becoming full of increasingly complicated music). Sometimes he failed to turn up at all, unable to connect with the music or the band of which he was a part, and if he did make that connection it was often only via a heroin fix that he could do so. Often he would lie backstage, watching the band but no longer a part of it.

It was during these dates that the frightening truth started to materialise, even on Hillel. "He was in terrible pain," Anthony later told *Behind The Music* on VH-1, "and that was the first time he realised he was in trouble with this thing, that it wasn't just a casual affair and it wasn't just for fun and it wasn't just a mind expanding trip. It had its meat hook in his heart and it wasn't letting go so easily."

Kiedis was to tell biographer Dave Thompson how he recognised in Hillel the addiction that he suffered from himself, the refusal to acknowledge the problem and the belief that he had control over it. While Kiedis' problems were evident to everyone around the band, Slovak was more discrete, but the two of them were both playing a dangerous game. While Anthony was happy to score in full view of his friends and colleagues, many members of the entourage *didn't even know* Hillel was using. No longer recreational, he was using heroin for deeply rooted needs of his own, not merely as one element of the party lifestyle that defined the band. To put such a problem into an ordinary person's ordinary day is bad enough – when placed in the context of rock and roll group on the edge of major success, with a gruelling touring schedule and work rate to match their ambition, this was clearly no place to kick or hide a habit.

Everybody wanted a piece of the Chili Pepper pie, and with fans, management, publishers and record companies all ready to lift the band to the next level, there was a huge sense of expectation and a huge pressure on individual band members. It is too easy to see this as expecting too much, placing undue pressure on Hillel and his colleagues. But it was only to be expected. The record companies are there to make money, they had stuck with the band through this many albums and were looking forward to a timely return on their investment, that was not abnormal; management and publishers too were only trying to steer the openly ambitious band towards greater and greater achievements; and the fans were simply getting off on the music and wanted to hear as much of it as possible. No one was to blame, everyone was just doing their job. The problem was, Hillel was falling apart. But the Chili Peppers were in danger of falling apart too.

For Flea and Kiedis, unquestionably the axis of power within the band, there was always the sense that this was *their* band, and that to lose it was to lose everything. Perhaps for Slovak, having once left the band and returned, this was not the case – it was less 'his' band, more 'the band he was in' – and he lost control too quickly? Who knows.

Then of course there are the people who are less honourable, less concerned with the health of the band and eager only to make a buck – the dealers. Rock and roll bands are the gravy trains of many drug dealers, they have the money to pay for the drugs, the contacts to get them and the itinerant lifestyle to reduce the risk of selling to them. Perfect punters. And so it was that like an army moving into town, the Chili Peppers attracted every major dealer in whatever city they played. After the gigs they would party on, in strip joints and other late night venues that could offer them some place to let their hair down and party. They had money to spend and attracted people around them like moths to a flame.

Before the untimely death of Kurt Cobain, there still lingered around the hard-living rock elite (to which the Chili Peppers now belonged) a strange air of the romantic about drug abuse and, in particular, heroin. The world's press tracked the increasing availability of crack across western cities, and this cheap and addictive version of cocaine was becoming a social problem throughout Europe and The United States, but for many older users, heroin remained the self-destruct weapon of choice. With 'heroin chic' a buzz term in advertising circles, Kurt and Courtney's private life was examined in intimate detail by the increasing scrutiny of not just the music journals but the general gossip-press of the world.

Following a gig in Washington the other members of the band thought that maybe it was time to let Slovak go: his playing, his lifestyle, his attitude and his addiction were dragging the band down. It was Angelo Moore of support act Fishbone who talked them into keeping him on, arguing that right now was when he needed them – his friends, his peer group – the most. He travelled to London for the Abbey Road sessions – more of which later - and the band's preparations for a European tour. Four weeks after returning home he was dead.

Around this time, a Chili Peppers roadie had approached Hillel's brother James and told him about his sibling's illness. "He said (Hillel) was doing heroin, but I didn't believe him at first," recalled James on VH-1. "He said you need to know it is getting out of hand. I confronted my brother and he begged me not to tell my mom. So I didn't. I would have told my mom if I had a second chance."

On a positive note, Anthony and Hillel had resolved to help each other clean up. "I mentioned it to Hillel," Anthony continued, "and we talked about it and I said we should both seriously think about being clean… we said we are both gonna perish, we're gonna lose the band. We thought we really should (clean up) 'cos we will have a lot more fun and we would make a lot more music and life will be better without it." Even Hillel's own diary revealed that he was fighting hard against his addiction, with one entry saying, "Fuck drugs, music is my diary."

Unfortunately, when they came off tour, as their manager Lindy Goetz explained to VH-1, they were separated and that strong resolve of being a pair of friends together against the heroin was dissipated: "They were trying to clean up and they were doing great. We'd been working very hard for a long time and they were fried. Everybody came home and said, 'hey, I'll go my way, you go your way and I will speak to you in three weeks.'" This period of isolation proved fatal, literally.

Kiedis had tried to communicate with his friend – he sent notes, scribbled messages, did everything to try and guide his pal back into line. Anthony lived for a long time with the knowledge that he had tried and failed to get through to Hillel – but that may be harsh on the lead singer as Hillel was probably not of the frame of mind for being helped. With the best will in the world, he even tried to get Slovak to join Alcoholics Anonymous, even though Hillel was not addicted to alcohol. But nothing could avert the inevitable.

Then Hillel's brother James received a phonecall from the guitarist. "He said he was thinking of doing heroin again," recalled James. Hillel also told James he loved him for the first time during that phonecall. However, it seems he put the phone down and scored straight away. "He knew he was going to do heroin that night, He was ashamed of it, I'm pretty sure," recalled James.

On Saturday night of June 27th, Slovak left his apartment to score, and, returning home alone, suffered an overdose. Slipping into a coma, he never woke up. Two days later a friend came by to see if he was okay and found his body on the floor of the apartment. Hillel Slovak died only 26 years old. He was buried five days later.

Anthony Kiedis' own descent into heroin abuse would later be charted on a song destined to become one of the best-known and most-loved tracks, 'Under The Bridge,' a Hendrix-esque confessional gem, written while Kiedis drove home from a rehearsal with the band. "I felt like I had no one," he said. "I felt like I had no friends… a feeling many junkies will be able to relate to." Sat in his car, desolate, lonely and afraid, he felt he understood how Slovak may have felt when he died, alone.

Anthony's mid-Eighties decline saw him hanging out with the wrong people on the wrong side of town, increasingly associating with characters from the LA drugs scene. Masquerading as a family member of one his contacts in order to be accepted, he found himself compromised in the way that so many addicts are. Hillel's death turned Kiedis around and led to his ultimate withdrawal from addiction in August of that year, but not before he had suffered beneath the literal and metaphorical bridge to which the song refers. Reluctant to identify the meeting place for fear that it may become some kind of misdirected shrine for junky rock fans, Kiedis has been at pains to explain that the bridge was real, that it was not the only place where he would meet to score or shoot up, but that it typified the squalor that had become to inhabit his inner life. In 2000 Kiedis told *Rolling Stone* that whatever situation he finds himself in – in particular threatening ones – he always has an 'innate sensation that says 'You're going to get out of this mess... It gives you carte blanche to explore areas you have no business going into..."

But Hillel hadn't shared this sense of Godspeed, of omnipotent protection somewhere out there. Now he was gone.

CHAPTER 7

In response to the death of their close friend and band member, Flea and Kiedis in particular found it hard to re-adjust. Kiedis simply vanished for a while, to an obscure Mexican village. "I did not accept the news. I was very much under the influence when I got it, my girlfriend told me and I refused to accept it." Surprisingly, Anthony continued to use heroin: "I didn't actually stop using at that point," he told VH-1, "you would think your best friend died, you would think, 'Okay, I've had enough,' but it doesn't work that way in my experience." Fortunately, ten days later he returned – much to Flea's relief – and checked into rehab, where he cleaned himself up.

Flea was equally devastated and later had this to say about Hillel's overdose: "He was going through a hard time and just made a mistake, took the wrong drugs at the wrong time and he didn't make it." Flea was distraught.

Irons, too, withdrew from everyday life, avoiding anything to do with the band. He had been Hillel's friend from years previous and the two had been inseparable. Now he was shattered. Finally accepted for psychiatric care in a mental hospital, Irons suffered a complete breakdown.

At this point in their career, and to all intents and purposes The Red Hot Chili Peppers could have died with Hillel right there in his apartment on that tragic night. Ironically, Hillel's death came during one of the happiest periods of Fleas's life. He later told *The Guardian*: "I was married and completely in love, and had a baby on the way," he said. "When Hillel died I completely hit the deck."

What had begun for Slovak as a creative adjunct, a little something to make the music flow more freely and the party run more smoothly, had become his killer. Like so many psychological problems unshared, the fact that Hillel had kept his addiction under wraps for so long – he couldn't tell his mother about it, and only when it was already too late found he could open up to his brother James – made it worse.

Talking to *Kerrang!* in 1990, Kiedis reflected that Hillel didn't die of an overdose, but he died of a disease, the disease of addiction. "In a strange way," he said, "we found strength from (his death)... It forced me to make a choice. I could either join Hillel or I could try and finish my life." "It should have been me," Kiedis told another journalist. "My propensity for over-the-edge indulgence was more renowned than his." Ironically, it was their shared involvement in excessive drug use that had put a gap between the life-long friends. Anthony called addiction a "bizarre and cunning enemy," an enemy beyond reason. Neither could bear to see the other in such a dislocated state. Flea, when he got the phone call bearing the news of a band member's death, immediately assumed that it was Kiedis who had succumbed.

Miraculously, after his trip south, Kiedis was apparently back in control of his life, returning from his self-imposed clean-up on August 1st. Flea's private life was improving too, enhanced by the arrival of a daughter. Some normality began to creep back into their lives. Clara Balzary was born to Flea and Loesha on September 17th, less than three months after the death of one of Flea's closest and oldest friend. Hillel had predicted the baby would be a girl. Her father had her name tattooed on his left arm, neatly between Jimi Hendrix and a chain of elephants. He and his wife also paid tribute to the new arrival in a less permanent way: "My daughter had just been born bald, she was bald little baby, so my wife and I we both shaved our heads for my daughter. We were all bald and people would see us and think we were really crazy. The funny thing is, it was one of the sanest times in my life because I was so focussed on being a family man and a good guy."

"We tried to use our loss as a bolstering, positive influence," Kiedis told the biographer Dave Thompson. Other members of the band made positive moves forwards too. The old order was breaking down and the original line-up of the band was gone for good. Could the band survive? How would the surviving members find a way forward? Of the original four members, one was dead, one lost to his own near-fatal addiction, and one – Jack Irons – completely broken. So began the next chapter of this remarkable soap opera. They were not finished: "We knew that we weren't done yet," said Anthony, "that the life of Red Hot Chili Peppers still had untapped creative energy that we didn't want to go to waste and that Flea and I were still best friends."

Slovak's death was a personal tragedy – obviously for his family and friends, but also for rock music, who lost an innovative and influencing force. Its other, longer term effect on the pop world, was to see the Chili Peppers regroup with a new line-up and a determination to turn the appalling few months behind them around. On behalf of their lost members, they would build this band back up, and turn it into something new.

RED HOT CHILI PEPPERS

Jack Irons never came home to the band that he helped to start. He spent time in a mental hospital following Hillel's death, and was clearly deeply wounded by his experiences. He was still resident there when he got a phone call from The Clash frontman Joe Strummer, inviting him to come join his band. He hadn't played the drums for six months: "You do know where I am don't you?" he asked Strummer. Typically, Joe persisted and talked Jack back behind the drum kit, and he played in Strummer's band for the best part of a year. Jack toured then with Red Cross, and formed the band Eleven as well as playing with Neil Young, but he never returned to the Peppers. In 1989 he met Eddie Vedder at one of Strummer's gigs, and the two became firm friends.

In 1990, Vedder joined Jack, Flea, and a bunch of others on a hiking trip in Yosemite National Park, where Flea nicknamed him Crazy Eddie. Some time early in their friendship, Irons gave Vedder a tape of a band he knew. They had asked him to join them on drums, and were looking for a vocalist, but Jack didn't want to move to Seattle, as they planned to do. Declining their offer, Jack thought that Crazy Eddie might be interested in the singer's job that was up for grabs. Vedder tracked the band down in Seattle. Joining Jeff Ament and Stone Gossard, with Mike McCready on guitar, 'Crazy Eddie' went on to form Pearl Jam, the nucleus of whom were on that tape handed over by Jack. The history of that band is, of course, another story – a story that Jack Irons came back into, when he joined Pearl Jam in 1994, and which he exited in 1998 due to health problems. For now, his part in the remarkable story of the Chili Peppers was over.

1988 was not the most notable year in UK pop history. Yazz, Kylie Minogue, Kim Wilde and Brother Beyond proved that there was little taste for radical experiment in the charts. Salt 'n' Pepa had a hit or two. A balding drummer from a Seventies prog rock band had a hit with a Sixties tune after he appeared in a film based on the Great Train Robbery. Fairground Attraction and The Proclaimers found a nice little niche for wistful Scottish folk. Michael Jackson made a load of money, and George Michael probably banked a lot more, but apart from that there wasn't much on the ground. What better time therefore, to release an EP on the cover of which four blokes would be seen dangling socks from their dicks?

In August, EMI released the Red Hot Chili Peppers' 'Abbey Rd' EP. Recorded in the UK before they returned to LA to prepare for the next album and tour – and crucially while Hillel was still alive – it was another step up the career ladder for the band. The disc cover was a fabulous parody of the original Beatles album sleeve (itself a classic of Sixties cool), which showed the four band members walking proudly across the pedestrian crossing outside EMI's world-famous north London studio wearing nothing but socks on their cocks. The idea to use 'Abbey Road' visually and as a title rather than just a recording venue was the idea of photographer Chris Clunn, though it wasn't exactly new. Since The Beatles, other bands had used the name of the famous studios as a marketing tool to promote a collection of songs, with George Benson's 'Other Side of Abbey Road' recreating the entire Beatles' album being a noted example. But the Chili Peppers' take was easily the... er... cheekiest of all. Oddly enough, in the Sixties all sorts of 'Paul is dead' rumours had surfaced, and some of the 'evidence' lay in the fact that on the cover of 'Abbey Road' McCartney wore no socks... a clear reference to some aged Tibetan death ritual (apparently). That the Peppers wore *only* socks (okay – there was a hat or two and some nifty footwear) was particularly entertaining. This must be a band both 'in' the tradition and outside it looking in, with a cool sense of irony and one hell of a nerve.

A modest Chris Clunn told *Kerrang!* that coming up with the idea "didn't take a brain surgeon." It was shot in February, and it was a freezing cold day: as they emerged from behind a bush (Abbey Road is a long, leafy, suburban road), the local commuters and pedestrians were stunned by this precocious bunch of tattooed Yanks prancing across the road. Clunn tells the entertaining story of how – having taken the shots – he got back home to realise that he had had no film in the camera. "I got a phone call about half six the following morning... They were on their way to the airport and stopped to do it again.... They jumped out of the minibus and we were finished in about ten minutes," he said. On the photos taken for the sleeve one can see cars approaching, one of them just pulling away from the kerb at the point where The Beatles' album showed a VW Beetle. God knows what the drivers and passengers were thinking.

The EP contained only one new song – a brave cover of Jimi Hendrix's 'Fire', which had been a live staple in the band's repertoire for a long time. The rest of the five-track collection started to sneak into the consciousness of the British audiences who had to this point still failed to really warm to the band. Their UK gigs were often poorly attended, and if anything their audiences were shrinking. Although the disc itself neither charted in

England nor sold particularly well for that matter, the back catalogue was looking healthier as the word spread about the foursome who had strode naked over the Abbey Road crossing.

In a way that was so typical of their careers – band highs arriving simultaneously with devastating lows and vice versa – back in LA, The Red Hot Chili Peppers were now without a drummer or a guitarist. Auditions came up with guitarist Duane 'Blackbyrd' McKnight – one of George Clinton's Funkadelic buddies. On drums they hired the former Dead Kennedy and Jello Biafra drummer DH Peligro ('Peligro' is the Spanish word for 'danger'!). Unfortunately, despite the tremendous credentials of these new recruits and everything that this band had done to keep going and stay working, it was obvious to Anthony and Flea that this was not the right group of people. Incredibly, only weeks after they joined, Peligro and McKnight were out. The band, in this incarnation, managed an appearance on MTV's *120 Minutes* show, but despite the apparent camaraderie, the former Fairfax High students were soon shopping for new members once again.

Bands often seem to only reach a certain level of success by going through a number of necessary changes. It seems that unless the pain and the uncertainty of those changes are met face-on then the band goes nowhere. It was just so for the Chili Peppers. Without the tragic death of Hillel and the 'don't blink or you'll miss me' residency of Blackbyrd McKnight, the band may never have found the man who ultimately would turn them from being nearly-men into a world-dominating supergroup.

Enter one John Frusciante...

CHAPTER 8

The man who effectively rescued the Red Hot Chili Peppers from potential disintegration was born on March 5th 1970 in New York. It's no exaggeration to call John Frusciante the 'soul' of the band. Kiedis may be its brains while Flea may be its ever-pounding heart, but without a soul the band would have died.

John's lawyer father was a classically-trained pianist and his mother Gail was a keen singer too (she appears on harmony vocals on 'Under The Bridge.') Like Kiedis before him, John moved to California when his parents separated: "Mom asked me if I wanted to move to LA. I said 'Yeah!' because I knew that was where the rock stars were. I was seven!" he said. Moving to Santa Monica (after spending time in Tuscon, Arizona and Florida en route), the kid was already starting to play guitar, and he has talked about how the voices that he heard as a junky were already in his head at this young age, responsible for him taking up the guitar in the first place. He even claims to have given the six string up because (even at this age) his standards were too high. Unable to play like Jimmy Page, he waited until punk rock re-lit his imagination, and by the age of ten could play his way through the whole of the Sex Pistols' *Never Mind The Bollocks*. Pretty soon John had mastered the styles of Jeff Beck and (finally) Jimmy Page, could emulate the terrifically complicated chords of UK progressive outfit King Crimson and its avant garde guitarist Robert Fripp – he could even knock off Genesis and Yes material for good measure. He learned Frank Zappa off by heart, and was proficient in copying Captain Beefheart and The Residents. He was intimately familiar with bands that had already shaped his future colleagues in the Chili Peppers – inspired by The Germs, a nine-year-old Frusciante had declared himself a punk rocker and worn out his copy of that band's *GI*. John has always improved his technique and playing – even to this day – by copying the work of other guitarists until he has made a part of their style a part of his own. It was clear to anyone with half an ear that John was a guitar talent of some considerable measure. This was not your average teenage guitar-playing rock fan.

Still a teenager when he auditioned for Frank Zappa's band, he left without completing the audition. "I realised that I wanted to be a rock star, do drugs and get girls," he told a reporter, "and that I wouldn't be able to do that if I was in Zappa's band." He was right to wait, as the band he was about to join could provide all three of these prerequisites in bucket-loads.

Fifteen when he fell in love with Slovak's guitar sound and the Chili Peppers in general, John first saw them play at Los Angeles' Variety Arts Center. Just as he was no ordinary guitarist, John was also no ordinary fan. He left home to follow the band on tour, and became a gig-buddy of the band, having been to so many shows. Even though he was broke as a teenager, Frusciante spent almost every dime he had on tickets to Chili Peppers shows, for himself and for friends. "Even then I thought they were the greatest band in the world, and that they could add beauty to anyone's life," he later told *Kerrang!* The band nicknamed him 'Greenie', because – well – he looked so young and green alongside everyone else. Impressed with his reputation as a guitar-protégé, they introduced him to West Coast band Thelonius Monster. Nervous as hell, Kiedis and Flea escorted the seventeen-year-old to the studio, and as they listened, they realised that here was the answer to all their prayers.

John was told he had passed the audition, and then to his amazement was further told that it had been for the Chili Peppers. Thelonius Monster or his favourite band of all-time? Who should he join? No contest. "Flea and Anthony called me and I kept real cool (when asked to join the band) but then I put the phone down and ran across the house and jumped up on the wall, there was these foot marks on the wall of the apartment!" John later recounted.

Slovak, who he would effectively be replacing, was his dream guitar player, and the lifestyle of his friends was most definitely the one that he wanted to live himself. Rumour had it that he also had to audition his erect dick to his future band-mates first. Presumably he passed this test too!

His work was immaculate – he could ape Slovak to perfection, but clearly had his own brand of explosive pyrotechnics. Anthony described 'Greenie' to the biographer Dave Thompson thus: "He's a very disciplined musician, all he cares about is his guitar and his cigarettes." If only John had stayed just caring about his cigarettes...

In an entertaining anecdote, Dave Thompson recalls a line from John on the subject of it becoming harder and harder to be a smoker in the USA because of the dangers of passive smoking. "If people are so worried about second-hand smoke," he said, "they should buy their own and stop using up everyone else's." By June 1999 however, both John and Anthony were off the cigarettes themselves and joining the ranks of the non-smoking world – 'going over to the enemy,' as John put it!

John Frusciante went on to turn the Red Hot Chili Peppers into the band that Flea and Kiedis had always dreamed it could, would and should be. Hillel Slovak was their friend and soul-brother, and his sound defined the group. Nobody else filled his shoes in the way that Frusciante did, and in this remarkable young man they found something of Hillel's core being as a person, as well as someone who could light their fire on stage and in the studio.

One audition down, one to go. With John on board, the new-style band was nearly complete, but they still needed someone who understood them like Jack Irons had, who could keep up with the lifestyle and who could party as well as he could drum. The search for a drummer was not as easy as for the new guitarist. Disillusioned with the thirty tub-thumpers that passed before them, it was at the end of a long and wearisome day that Chad Smith walked in, screamed as many obscenities as he hit fabulous rhythms, and took over the Irons/Peligrew drum position without question. Kiedis likened his performance to "a herd of psychedelic gorillas."

The story is reminiscent of the one told by Pete Townsend, then auditioning drummers for his yet-to-be-famous band The Detours, who went on to be better known as The Who. Townsend told the BBC how, after a similar day of plodding drummers marching through the rehearsal rooms, in came a guy with ginger hair, wearing ginger clothes from head to toe and carrying a pint of (ginger-coloured!) pale ale. He promptly smashed the kit to pieces with a firework display of drumming that put all the others in the shade. The Who had found their drummer, Keith Moon.

In a similar way, Kiedis was immediately impressed by Chad. He also tells the story of how they told their metal-head new drummer to cut his hair before he could join officially. In no uncertain terms he declined their suggestion and by proving to be more punk than the punks themselves, with an uncompromising self-confidence and 'fuck you' attitude, he was the last piece in the newly-completed Chili Pepper jigsaw. In stark contrast to John, Chad didn't know the Chili Peppers' albums at all, but in an interview Flea outlined the criteria for success in the band, and Chad seems to have fitted perfectly from day one: "If (a player has) no rules, no limits to what they do, and they have a love for music, especially funk music (Author's note: okay, almost perfect), that they're able to express through their playing, then they'll probably fit right in with the Red Hot Chili Peppers."

RED HOT CHILI PEPPERS

Chad Smith was born on October 25th, 1962 in St Pauls, Minnesota, a metal freak and champion drummer of several pre-Chili Pepper bands, including RCA-released Toby Redd, who retain a live following to the present day. Chad has returned to the Toby Redd drum stool on numerous occasions for reunion gigs and one-offs, and has even retained a Toby Redd dressing room at Chili Peppers' gigs!

A truant from school, Chad was a runaway at fifteen years of age, when he spent a summer sleeping in cars and crashing in other people's homes, accompanied by a dog called Bong. On his return home, his mother ensconced him in a Catholic boarding school, but Chad was never a settled pupil, smoking pot and hanging out, but not attending many lessons. After school, Smith was a veteran employee of pancake houses, paint companies and GAP stores (he was fired from all three) before finding his niche as one of the world's most influential drummers.

Smith injected a sense of musical security – he simply liked to drum and he hit those things *hard*. Indeed, a friend of the band had alerted them to Smith telling them "I know this guy from Detroit, he eats drums for breakfast!" A true, bike-riding, bandana-sporting rocker, beyond drumming he didn't take life *too* seriously.

Despite their new drummer claiming not to know a single one of their songs, The Red Hot Chili Peppers were a fighting unit once more. Refreshed, renewed and with the flames of their blitzkrieg new line-up still fresh in the fire, they hit the road. (Notably, Flea and John had a temporary diversion with their band Hate and the former had also been moonlighting as a trumpet player with Trulio Disgracias.)

Kicking off in March 1989, nine months after Hillel's death, the tour marked a new beginning for the band. As it progressed, the kind of trouble that the band increasingly attracted started to unfold. For starters, Kiedis was arrested after a complaint from a woman at a gig. Anthony admitted that in his dressing room after a show at George Mason University, "I was changing and there was a girl there. We were all joking together and when she left no one was under the impression that she was perturbed by my nudity in the dressing room." However, 24 hours later, she filed a complaint and he was charged with two misdemeanour counts. He strongly denied the charges, but was found guilty the following year of 'indecent exposure' (for which he paid a fine; he appealed against the other charge of sexual battery). Ironically, this was a particularly stable and sober period in Kiedis' life. He had been dating actress Ione Skye, the daughter of Sixties folk/pop guru Donovan and he had to all intents and purposes dropped his womanising ways, given up cigarettes, booze and drugs, and was living the life of a reformed man.

Ione was sixteen-years-old when the couple had first got together at a launch party for *Uplift Mofo Party Plan*. She moved in with Kiedis shortly afterwards, and told a teen magazine that the couple spent most of their time curled up with their pet dog watching old Vivien Leigh and Bette Davis movies. For his part, Anthony described Ione as "one of the most ultimate angelic creatures on Earth." Sadly, the angel left him over Christmas 1989, marrying and then divorcing Adam Horowitz from The Beastie Boys, but the couple retained a friendship. Eleven years later they co-hosted a fashion benefit show in aid of women suffering from alcohol and drug addiction. Anthony had made real steps in sorting his wild lifestyle out. Aside from his arrest and conviction, or otherwise, he nevertheless was a far more stable being than he had been a year previously.

After her time with Anthony, Skye publicly revealed her bisexuality, and Kiedis wryly recounted for one interviewer the problems that this entailed: "I've been in bed with a girl, and she'll be like, 'You know, that last person I had sex with was your ex-girlfriend.' I'm like, 'Well – you don't say!'"

The tour itself was another step up for the band, who continued to court controversy at the same rate that they continued to put their house back in order. They pumped the music out for virtually two years up to the recording of forthcoming new album *Bloodsugarsexmagic*, endlessly crossing America and travelling the world. Audiences greeted their blend of funk and rock with an ecstatic response, and anticipation for the next album was high. Three superb singles – 'Knock Me Down', 'Taste The Pain' and 'Higher Ground' (a Stevie Wonder cover) whetted the appetite of band and fans alike for the forthcoming album. Lying on their backs, heads together and legs splayed, the band re-created their asterisk logo in the video for 'Higher Ground.' Low budget and fun, the video features friends and family of the band, called in to appear in the group-hug and dancing scenes, while the endless array of hallucinogenic images in the background were the work of a long-term friend. Scattering psychedelic images blend with stock footage and almost Jackson Pollock-like pictures. One highlight of the video was the pair of trousers worn by Flea – made almost entirely from stuffed toy animals!

RED HOT CHILI PEPPERS

This was quite clearly a new dawn, a burst of creative energy with a new guitar player who instinctively knew what was best for the band, although he was some eight years younger than his fellow players.

CHAPTER 9

Michael Beinhorn returned to the studio with the Chili Peppers to develop an album more melodic than before, destined to appeal to the legions of fans who had followed their live set throughout the previous spring. Keidis explained that they were searching for a genre-free groove, a music that stood on its own: "like a few people: Bob Marley, John Lennon, Miles Davis." Quite a standard to aspire too then. It is interesting that Keidis quotes a reggae legend, a songwriting pop rocker and a jazz institution – no heavy rock, no funk.

By rights, the next album, *Mother's Milk* should never have been made. The passing of Hillel Slovak had impacted on the band irrevocably. Yet more time was taken recruiting first John Frusciante and the Chad Smith but, fortunately for the Chilis, EMI were satisfied enough with *The Uplift Mofo Party Plan*'s US chart placing that they were encouraging in the band straightening themselves out to make another record.

The addition of Smith and Frusciante provided a new focus for the founder members, a second bite at the cherry after a catastrophic turn of events. *Mother's Milk*, the new fruits of their collective labour and the re-launching of the band, was an album all about *focus*.

Another celebratory, all-in-it-together funk rock anthem, 'Good Time Boys' could almost have been lifted *The Uplift Mofo Party Plan*. Slickly-produced and, once again, bigging-up the power of the Chili Peppers union despite the change in the ranks, the band were jamming harder than ever. But just when the rock world was awash with bass-slapping goons in tie-dye, the band were moving away from a genre with a limited life-span. Their musical tastes had always been all-encompassing anyway, their reference points widespread – Sixties, Seventies and Eighties punk and metal had all vied for space in the mix, only now were the band able to focus on drawing these disparate sounds together.

Ironically, it was the band's inspired cover version of Stevie Wonder's 'Higher Ground' that broke the band. The lead single off the album, the band retained all the qualities of the original, but rocked it up with big guitars, Flea's bouncing bass and Smith's drums resonated as if they were sheets of metal. The end result was a chunk of burning funk with a speedcore finale, straightforward enough for rock radio. 'Subway To Venus' – the title alone was a typically thinly veiled sexual metaphor – was a frisky, horn-laden song in the vein of early material, but somehow so much sharper. It would feature heavily in the set each night on the band's forthcoming world tour. The band had all been lifelong LA Lakers fans and 'Magic Johnson' was their tribute to their greatest player, a tongue-twisting rant set to a frantic signature Smith drum beat. A tribute to another player, Kareem Abdul-Jabbar, was recorded but didn't make the final album cut.

'Nobody Weird Like Me' was an anthem for freaks, deviants and rock and roll underdogs everywhere and the first song Frusciante had played with the band during their initial rehearsals together. Vocoders, squealing guitars and some of the fastest playing by Flea yet made for a metal riff pile-up. 'Knock Me Down' was the band's tribute to Hillel Slovak, a heart-warming warning shot. Ultimately though 'Knock Me Down' managed to sidestep dour sentimentality and remain upbeat, the sign of a band with a rediscovered lust for life. Slow-burning and paranoid-sounding 'Taste The Pain' was experimental by Chili's standards and something of a strange choice for a single (in the UK). The hard-hitting 'Stone Cold Bush' was another typical celebration of the female anatomy.

Along with Stevie Wonder, *Mother's Milk* also saw the band worshipping at the temple of another of their gods: Jimi Hendrix. 'Fire' was one of Hendrix's most instantly gratifying songs and band did it justice by putting the pedal to the metal and playing at breakneck speed, Slovak's guitar was featured from beyond the grave on the latter track along with Jack Irons on drums (one of Slovak's paintings graced the sleeve). 'Pretty Little Ditty' was a beautiful – and some would say much-needed – interlude from the funked-up thrashing madness, John Frusciante showing just why the band could hardly believe their luck in finding a such an amazing undiscovered talent, as the song builds to a trumpet crescendo, courtesy of Flea, naturally. The lilting guitar riff from the song was later sampled and turned into a hit by rap-metal pretenders Crazy Town.

'Punk Rock Classic' was a caustic sideswipe at those contemporaries happy to conform and adapt to MTV and corporate radio's needs. The Chili Peppers weren't exactly doyens of the underground (indeed they'd be all over for MTV for the next decade) but the song was written by a band still waiting for the big break. 'Sexy Mexican Maid' was a slow-grinding straightforward sex fantasy complete with saxophone solo and co-written with DH Peligro. A surprisingly edgy but somewhat tuneless conclusion to the *Mother's Milk* party, 'Johnny, Kick A Hole In The Sky' began with an out-of-tune rendering of the 'Star Spangled Banner' and ended the album with a bang. Lyrically, it saw the band in another rare moment of political clarity. Despite the ups and downs of their career to date, all those heartbreaks and disappointments, the Red Hot Chili Peppers' politics still consisted of one maxim: fuck it, let's party. *Mother's Milk* was the album to take the party to the world.

'Knock Me Down', the tribute to Hillel, was released as the first single in his memory, its success in comparison with earlier releases clearly indicated that a new audience was out there and ready for the band. The album sold well, and their singles and tours were increasingly high profile.

'Taste The Pain' and 'Higher Ground' followed the Slovak tribute as the next single, warming up the world for the forthcoming album. 'Show Me Your Soul' featured on the soundtrack to the hit Julia Roberts/Richard Gere movie *Pretty Woman*, and subsequently became a hit single in the UK. Suddenly, or so it seemed, it was all looking good again.

The cover shot for the album featured model Dawn Alaine, who complained that the band had not had permission to use the shot, the design being Anthony's own concept. The cover shot caused problems for some retailers in the United States, who wanted to stock large quantities of the album but were worried by the visibility of Dawn's breasts. The band denied that they were selling out by agreeing to amend the cover.

This was a fun-loving band, they rode close to the edge in everything they did. Nobody suggested that the album cover was intentionally provocative, but if it did raise the hackles of a handful of prurient buyers, then the maxim is: 'there's no such thing as bad publicity.' Two versions of the cover exist – the first, more common one, shows John on Dawn's arm, whereas on the rarer release he appears on her shoulder. Likewise, Chad's squatting pose changes, and in the shot Flea wears a baseball cap missing from the other version. The album carried an 'explicit lyrics' sticker, and while we might expect the band to have derided this move, in fact Anthony welcomed it. "Our lyrics are very explicit," he told *Kerrang!* "If they wanna inform the buying public that it's explicit, I have no problem."

The back cover of the *Mother's Milk* showed a painting of a naked woman. It was the work of Hillel Slovak, and beneath the picture a dedication referred to the lost brother, the soul mate who had paid the ultimate price in his service to the band. The biggest irony of all was that this was an album that took one more giant leap forward. Although their guitarist was barely out of nappies and their drummer, by his own admission, didn't know the songs that they had released previously, it was a devastatingly good album. Rather than slow the band down, the fresh blood of Frusciante and Smith injected a new pace and a revived attack into their music. The powerful characters of Flea and Kiedis were destined for stardom: their charisma has maintained sideline careers in movies and guaranteed column inches and photo shoots. With *Mother's Milk,* the music caught up with them, and they could claim to be famous for all the right reasons – theirs was a cracking good band.

Carrying the burden of the previous months, Kiedis was not ready to give up on sex as a prime source of inspiration, but he clearly achieved a level of maturity in his performance and writing unprecedented so far. Exciting, volatile, *Mother's Milk* was above all, patently commercial. Whereas previously they had been hard to categorise – part-rock band, part-funk band, part-punk etc – they could now be re-categorised as the part-rock, part-funk, part-punk band with a platinum album on their hands. Without compromising anything, the Red Hot Chili Peppers had made a record for *everyone.*

As for the title, *Mother's Milk* , Anthony told Dave Thompson that the properties of breast milk – its ability to nurture and build strong bones, its loving warmth – were chosen as an image because they felt their music represented all the same qualities. What a lovely thought – until you realise that (as he also told Thompson) they had considered calling the album *Rocking Freakapotamus.* Presumably that title would have represented something else... though fans will recognise it as the name of the official fan club.

A couple of entertaining anecdotes came out of the above-mentioned *Mother's Milk* track 'Magic Johnson'. All the members of the band are big basketball fans, and Magic Johnson, of the Los Angeles Lakers, is Anthony and Fleas' big hero. Chad, however, is a Detroit Pistons fan, convinced that Johnson sold out when he left his hometown of Lansing, Michigan, to play in California. The band recorded Smith's contribution to the song without telling him who, or what, it was about, and only afterwards did he discover that he had helped create a tribute to the star. The band took to flooding the stage with lighting based upon the Lakers yellow and purple colours, and Chad has to sit through the ignominy of his contribution to the homage every time they play. Flea and Anthony finally got to meet their hero, who was singularly unimpressed with them and with the track, and on MTV – when they told the tale – you could see that their rejection had hurt.

A similar brush with a hero of the movie world had disappointed the guys when – at a Lakers game – Anthony bumped into actor Jack Nicholson. Anthony asked Jack if he would pass a copy of the song onto 'Magic' for him. Jack dismissed Anthony (calling him 'kid'!) out of hand, denying that he knew Johnson, and waved him away. "Fuck, what an asshole," Anthony told *Penthouse* when he recounted the tale for them. "Later… I realised – what else could he do?" No matter how famous you are, there's always someone who doesn't know you and doesn't care! The last laugh in the whole tale may yet be Chad's, who claims that if you play the song backwards you can hear the chant "LA sucks! LA sucks!" from one of the bands' out of town concerts. Allegedly.

Never a band to plug themselves too quietly, T-shirt merchandise from the *Mother's Milk* tour showed Madonna apparently masturbating to the album. "I think if she saw it, she'd want one," Anthony told Mick Wall of *Kerrang!* Thousands of these shirts were sold on the hilariously-named 'Positive Mental Octopus' tour which covered Europe and America. Of particular note was the night they found themselves playing to a huge audience in Dam Square in Amsterdam. Parliament singer Michael 'Clip' Payne joined the band on backing vocals and Keith Chapman on sax. The physical demands of so many shows took its toll on Anthony in particular. Kiedis spent much of his time on tour hobbling around on crutches or nursing his bruises – until show time, when his acrobatic and self-destructive stage antics (responsible for the above injuries!) were phenomenal.

On a more serious note, other opportunities for self-destruction were avoided at all costs: the death of Hillel was still fresh in everyone's minds, and drugs were banned from the tour. This did not mean, however, that they had lost their sense of mischief. In the UK, booked to appear on the *Jonathan Ross* TV show, the band declared that it would only play if they were allowed to play naked. When this was politely declined they agreed to continue only if Flea was suspended upside down for the entire performance. The producers of the show agreed, and the bass player hung from a rope while Anthony leapt over Ross's desk and ran wild in the audience.

RED HOT CHILI PEPPERS

Things didn't calm down much back in the States, when Flea was charged with various misdemeanours, allegedly having simulated sexual acts with a bikini-clad audience member at the MTV Spring Break Party in Daytona, Florida. Booked to lip-sync to 'Knock Me Down' for a forthcoming video release, Flea fell off Anthony's shoulders during a bout of fooling around, and grabbed at the nearest thing to hand. Unfortunately that turned out to be a girl, who Flea promptly picked up, threw over his shoulder, and began to spin around while Chad spanked her. Flea and Smith were arrested two days later (according to *Q Encyclopaedia of Rock Stars* they pleaded guilty to battery and paid fines which went to a rape crisis centre); most definitely an unwelcome diversion for the band. "Most people who come to our shows understand that there's a humour element to what we do," Anthony said later. "The first amendment on the American Constitution gives you the freedom of speech and the freedom – you know – to do what you will from the stage!" That said, the right- wing groups who were constantly tracking the band's activities were delighted to be given such ammunition with which to once again criticise the group and it was, for all its innocence, an unfortunate turn of events in an otherwise super-charged and progressive period of the band's career.

Whatever the American Constitution had to say, Flea and Chad were found guilty. Both guys admitted that they had got carried away, and showed appropriate contrition for what they had done. Perhaps it was just time for the authorities to make an example of the band, in the same way that the Rolling Stones were singled out and hounded by London's drug squads in the Sixties, despite virtually every musician in town being involved in drug-taking to some degree.

At another gig at Green Bay they were again arrested – but later released without charge – for alleged indecent exposure. Cleaner-living in the narcotics sense, this was a band clearly high on something, as their frolics on and off stage became more and more unpredictable and entertaining. Perhaps because of that, the band were undoubtedly becoming some kind of target for the authorities, and it was clear that they would have to watch out in the future or eventually get busted big time – perhaps even for something they hadn't done. Flea expressed his own concerns that – now the father of a three-year-old daughter – he should not be represented as some woman-baiting hell raiser. Still a punk rocker at heart, he still felt the right to give the finger to society if it deserved it, but also sensed the responsibilities that fatherhood entailed.

But clearly the band was becoming big enough that attacks on them by critics could often be turned into positive publicity. When they ran off the rails, instead of the kind of Chili Pepper-bashing they used to endure they now were treated to a flurry of media interest. EMI released a video from the *Mother's Milk* tour to cash in on the increased success of the band (or, if you like, to give the increasing number of their fans a slice of the tour as a memento). *Psychedelic Sex Funk From Heaven* is three-quarters of an hour of live footage from the tour, intercut with behind-the-scenes footage, an honest testament of the band in their glory and on the brink of major-league success. with Flea resplendent in a red cheerleaders mini skirt, and playing 'The Star Spangled Banner' on his trumpet.

Despite the increasing success, there was anxiety in the band. Kiedis and Beinhorn were rumoured to be not getting on, Frusciante was unhappy with his own playing. The continued pressures of fatherhood meant that Flea, too, was uncomfortable in his rock and roll star skin. Anthony summed it up this way: "Living in Los Angeles and doing what I do, it's very easy to get wrapped up like an onion with a million layers of bullshit, and completely lose touch with your inner core,"

The band decided it was time to move record labels. Despite their new-found success with EMI, they apparently felt that they were under-promoted, and announced that they would be looking for a new home as their contract expired. Typically, they posed for photographs with the president of Sony outside that company's offices, only at the last minute to decide against the deal and sign with Warner Bros. Mo Austin, the legendary Warner president, called each member of the band individually and talked them out of discussions with Sony and into his own company. Rumoured to have been worth ten million bucks, the Warner deal was clearly the big step-up for the band. Whatever happened next, The Red Hot Chili Peppers were going to be huge.

In 1990, Anthony gave a major interview to *Kerrang!* magazine in the wake of the release of *Mother's Milk*. Journalist Mick Wall expected to find Kiedis in unpredictable mood, but when the singer leapt over the third floor balcony only to hang there by his fingertips complaining that he was bored, he realised that there was still something intriguingly vital about the guy. On stage and on film a bronzed Adonis, stripped to his muscular waist (or beyond), in the flesh Mick Wall found Anthony to be a young-looking, slight man, even-tempered and quietly spoken. Although the conversation was restrained, its subject matter was far from it. Kiedis expounded on the need to care for the environment, told the tales of his recent arrests and fines. He talked of how he was fined $1000 on each count of his arrest at George Mason University. He was reticent to discuss the matter at length, but animated on the subject of Madonna masturbating! "That's the kind of girl she is," he said. Most interestingly, Anthony spoke carefully about what the Chili Peppers image as rampant sex-fiends fuelled by lust and drugs meant to him. "This is showbusiness, and we are here to entertain," he said, demonstrating that the lessons learned at the knee of his movie-lifestyle father had not been wasted all those years ago. Ironically, some people took the band so seriously that they emulated them in their own careers. On the subject of Faith No More's Mike Patton – who as mentioned above had been cited as one such copycat - Anthony jokingly said that Chad Smith was preparing to kidnap him, shave his hair off and amputate one of his feet for copying Kiedis hook line and sinker. But the singer was philosophical: "He's just a kid," he admitted. "Besides, without his left foot…"

Ever the businessman beneath the wild rock image, Kiedis was confident that despite his dislike for the climate and diet, his band would soon be as big in Europe as they were rapidly becoming at home. He compared developing a market to the process of making love to somebody (perhaps one of his more bizarre sex metaphors!) – a slow but delicious process of teasing and pleasing until finally…bang! Sex was high on the interview agenda: recently established with a new girlfriend, Anthony was on a 'sex diet' – low fat for energy and aesthetics – at least this was refreshing and a far cry from the narcotics and booze of only a year or so before. Anthony has always been proud of his 'healthy' attitude to sex. He seems free from hang-ups and claims that his upbringing in his father's liberal home is to be thanked. "Sex is a simple and natural function of life," he says, "and to deny it, or be afraid of it… is something that ends up causing psychological ailments."

CHAPTER 10

By the time they came to record their new album in 1991, the majority of the band were hitting thirty and in fine mental and physical shape. The success of *Mother's Milk* (the band's first album to go gold and it stayed in the US *Billboard* charts for over *eight* months) and the subsequent two years of touring and promotion had unified a group who had started the cycle as fifty per cent strangers.

A new record label and a new album meant a new producer for the band. Rick Rubin, the co-founder of Def Jam Recordings, was a key figure in the development of hip-hop. His blend of rap and metal punched a hole in the compartmental world of pop where crossovers were often derided and unsuccessful. The Beastie Boys' *Licensed To Ill* and Run DMC's *Raising Hell* were landmark albums produced by Rubin, who also put together one of the most influential albums of the entire era, Public Enemy's debut *Yo! Bum Rush the Show*. Freed from Def Jam after a split with partner Russell Simmons, Rubin – a burly, heavily-bearded figure – was available to put the final touches to the re-invention of the Chili Peppers as 'biggest act in the world.' This wasn't their first meeting – as mentioned above, Rubin had met them while Slovak was still alive, but the drug culture around the band ("they were really in bad shape," Rubin said) put him off. This time they were ready for each another. Rick Rubin had caught the final show of the *Mother's Milk* world tour and had been blown away. The dark cloud he had seen hanging over them during that first awkward meeting had lifted to unveil a world-beating band, primed and hungry to step things up a notch – and he was just the man to guide them. "They didn't really fit into the category of any band that I had dealt with before," he later said, "and I thought it would be great fun to make – and it was."

The band used a rehearsal space called Alleyway, run by a pair of hippy-bikers. Surrounded by Seventies memorabilia and artefacts, the band quickly had something going on with virtually every riff they played or every note in Kiedis' lyric book. Rubin came to rehearsals and quietly figured out the dynamic of the band and came to understand their music. He allowed them room to experiment, to find new facets in their playing or writing, and gently encouraged Kiedis' own lyric-writing. It was Rubin who talked Anthony into bringing the un-realised 'Under The Bridge' into rehearsal for the first time: "I got to Anthony's house to discuss lyrics with him," recalled Rubin on VH-1's *Behind The Music* "and he showed me 'Under The Bridge'. I could just tell he was opening his heart, they were beautiful words. It wasn't a song yet, it was just words on a page but you could tell they were special." The problem was that Anthony was *very* nervous about presenting the poem to his band mates. His style of vocals were hardly best suited to acoustic, unplugged renditions; also, he had been clean of drugs for some time so this was a sober man singing about an experience that was entirely related to drug use, something he found incredibly personal. So it took some persuasion of an under-confident Chili Pepper singer to get him to drive over to the studio with the poem. He needn't have worried: "I hadn't done drugs for a few years… so I went in there and sang it to them and I probably sang out of tune and used three keys at the same time, but instead of laughing, they heard what I was trying to do they just went to their instruments and started playing."

He continued, "I was so nervous that my voice cracked when I tried to sing it (but) the band listened to every last word." Within minutes, the essence of what would become the Chili Peppers biggest song to date was complete.

'Give It Away' harked back to Anthony's former girlfriend Nina Hagen, the cult German musician, whose collaborations in the late Seventies brightened up the dimly–lit corners of the UK punk revolution. Aged twenty when the pair went out, Kiedis had been impressed by Hagen's principal that the more she gave away, the more she would always receive. Kiedis conceived the concept that sobriety depended upon something being given up in order for it to be maintained, and – on a sweaty summer day – the song was rooted around one of Flea's most memorable bass riffs.

Eschewing the sterility of many of LA's favoured state-of-the-art hi-tech studios, Rubin invited them to his home to record the follow-up to *Mother's Milk*. Hence they convened in May 1991 at Rubin's out-of-town hacienda off Mulholland Drive. Built upon the site of Harry Houdini's former home, and allegedly the scene of the Beatles' first acid trip, the location was a key part of the success of the sessions. Bringing recording equipment in from outside, Rubin isolated the band from the rest of the world in a house where different values were at play. Show-boating was kept to a minimum and Kiedis, while still playing the role of oversexed king of the urban jungle was, thanks to a new found awareness after cleaning up from heroin, beginning to show that the feelings in his heart were as powerful as those in his loins. They lived together for two months, claiming not to have fought or fallen out once. It has passed into Chili Pepper legend that everyone on the project felt that the house was haunted. Chad actually voted to stay at his own nearby home in the end, unwilling to share his room with a bunch of ghouls, but a medium confirmed that the ghosts were a friendly presence, and the band continued with the sessions. It may have also had a slight influence on at least three quarters of the band that Magic Johnson was also a neighbour.

A typical day would begin just after what most people would consider lunch-time. Rising at 1pm, work would begin an hour or so later. Creative, focussed, the sessions were fun too, as the later-to-be-released *Funky Monks* video would show. Frusciante told of how the creative process often gave him a hard-on, but that "I try not to ejaculate… I think if I ejaculate it will be to the detriment of the music."

The making of *Bloodsugarsexmagik* was documented in this short film, later released on video – the title clearly reference to their round-the-clock devotion and all-round sense of Trappist detachment in making the album. The film provided a valuable insight into Planet Chili Pepper - from their approach to their philosophy (cue plenty of odd rambles from Mr. Frusciante) to how they individually choose to spend their down-time on camera: Kiedis discussing his personal troubles, Smith riding his beloved 'hog' down the freeway.

Indeed, Smith became almost a link to the outside world for the rest of the group. Instead of being entirely isolated, the other three found a route to reality through Chad, who would come into work each day on his motor bike like some regular guy at the office. Frusciante and Flea gave up shaving during the sessions, and competed to grow the most extreme sideburns. The whole business was set up like some boxing promotion amongst the crew and band, with Flea and John each having a manager in Chad and Anthony. Flea won – the man with the magnificent chops! Evidence from *Funky Monks* showed that Anthony underwent acupuncture treatment during the making of the album, helping him deal with his more self-destructive tendencies. The film also shows the two-year-old Clara Balzary trying to scrub away her dad's tattoos in the bath, a touching scene of the proud dad and his lovely little girl. The kid was comfortable around the band and its associates. She would happily paint with Frusciante and would be left with drum tech and Bicycle Thief drummer Chris Warren when dad needed a baby sitter.

RED HOT CHILI PEPPERS

Funky Monks was directed by Flea's brother-in-law Gavin Bowden, over May and June, an hour-long, black and white exploration of the band in the middle of the creative process. River Phoenix appears briefly, alongside Rick Rubin and other key players in the making of the album, and the film trails them around the domestic hours of the day as well as the creative ones. Deeply philosophical in parts, it is equally silly and funny in others – for some the best of the official Chili Pepper videos.

Yet, *Funky Monks* is in a way a spooky gloss over the band's past and future. The band was gradually leaving the death of Hillel Slovak behind and was on the very verge of major fame. The fun and frolics, the studio antics and moments of musical magic: they are all part of a present that, in retrospect, seems so transitory. *Kerrang!* put it rather nicely: "It's watching John Frusciante's enthusiasm and sheer excitement at being in his favourite band that is rather heart-breaking, given the appalling depths to which he would descend." In fact it wasn't long after completing these album sessions that John first started to get into heroin.

With private security and an ex-Playboy centrefold as house cook, the band recorded tracks live, Rubin getting nearer than other producers in capturing what it was that burned when the band played on stage in front of a live audience. They had been on the road for so many months promoting *Mother's Milk* that they were in as good a shape musically as they could possibly have been in. In several 20-hour long sessions, Rubin found a route to their camaraderie on tour, as well as ways to keep their playing as relaxed and inspirational as it was on stage. One way of doing this was on the Robert Johnson cover 'They're Red Hot,' which was recorded outside the hacienda amidst the local traffic noise, all feeling of studio angst removed. Chad drummed with his hands, the others chilled out on acoustic guitar; while John's mum, as previously mentioned, joined the backing vocals for 'Under The Bridge.' This was a band who had clearly found – or been shown by Rubin – how to chill out, how to take the sheen of performance craft off the top of their songs, and how to get to the core both of what they wanted to say on this album and to how they wanted to say it.

Kiedis talked about how easily the music came to them. Flea remarked upon how his bass playing was becoming more simplified, how he found that to leave more space in his style gave more resonance to what he did play. One result of this was that he certainly left more space for Frusciante's guitar to find its own tone. John found that he no longer listened to, nor cared about what he played – he simply enjoyed the process of making music with people he loved.

The actual album itself, when completed, was an undoubted modern classic, an over-used phrase but one that is truly applicable here. 'The Power Of Equality' upheld the tradition of kicking off with a funked-up bang. All shimmering Hendrix guitars, Kiedis rapping and a fine Sly Stone-style chorus, it's testament to the quality of the album that followed in saying it was far from the strongest track. The best was yet to come. 'If You Have To Ask' was part-Prince, part…well, Chili Peppers. Frusciante and Smith were now comfortably a part of the band sound as Slovak and Irons once were, and that sound was now an instantly recognisable one. The young guitarist stamped his mark all over the record with a blistering solo which drew a round of applause on the song itself. The band left it in. He deserved it.

Opening with some rare acoustic guitars, 'Breaking The Girl' was a tribute to Kiedis' mother Peggy and an account of his time living with his father, Blackie. It was a rare moment of introspection and mellow pan-pipes. For the percussive middle section the band the acquired parts of old cars from a nearby junkyard and bashed out their rhythms al fresco like a prehistoric tribe of nomads transplanted into the twentieth century.

'Funky Monks' was lowdown funk, mid-paced and swaggering under the weight of its own inherent *badness*. It seemed to capture the mood of organic music and communal Laurel Canyon living perfectly. The band was partying hard, only this time without the aid of addictive chemicals. Weed and booze yes, but not heroin. 'Suck My Kiss' was one of the biggest party songs of them all – an essential component of what could be termed the Chili's erection section: those songs guaranteed to fill the dance floor and get any room moving. 'Suck My Kiss' showed the band at their muscular best, as they locked down on a beat and offered some fine tongue-in-cheek fighting talk. Unsurprisingly given its flab-free sounds and sharp hooks, day-time radio fell for the song in a big way and it was soon transcending all genres and become an outright hit.

The accompanying video for when this track was released as a single helped reinforce the Chili Peppers growing status as an MTV essential band. Gavin Bowden's video clip for 'Suck My Kiss' showed the house in which *Bloodsugarsexmagik* was recorded, featuring the band in recording sessions and at play. Interestingly, it intercut with scenes from the homecoming parade of troops from the first Gulf War, military aircraft overhead and a huge heart drawn in sky-writing. The blend of at-home band images and military celebration was an unusual concept, but illustrated America's ability to turn everything into a parade.

Back on the album itself, the band was shifting between styles artfully and with confidence. 'I Could Have Lied', for example, was stripped-down and plaintive but illuminated by a breathtaking Frusciante solo, before big riffs kicked back in to dominate the terminally groovy 'Mellowship Slinky in B Major', as Kiedis name-checked some of his heroes including writers such as Charles Bukowski, Truman Capote, Mark Twain and controversial artist Robert Williams, in amongst the usual sexual imagery ("pink umbrellas", for one). Despite Frusciante cranking it up on 'The Righteous And The Wicked' with a metallic solo, the song fails to keep up with the stiff competition – namely the song which followed it, 'Give It Away'.

Beginning life as a typical Chili free-flowing jam, 'Give It Away' morphed into a monster song and another career highlight for the band. If they had generally been a bass-led entity this far, then this song was pinnacle of Flea's influence – his loping, flexing bass lines dropping away to reveal a groin-grabbing, ass-shaking chorus that was everything good about the band: ridiculously funky, flagrantly sexy. It was also one of few hit singles to feature a guitar solo played backwards. And as lead tracks went, the dark Seventies space funk of 'Blood Sugar Sex Magik' was worthy of the album title.

Of all the songs the Chili Peppers had recorded in their first decade as a band, though, 'Under The Bridge' turned them into *bona fide* superstars. This song was written about the time Kiedis spent wrestling with heroin addiction and the comfort to be found walking the familiar city streets of his hometown. The song is both a warm-sounding open letter yet carries a message of loneliness through addiction where only the inanimate and the judgemental provide solace. It straddled the genres of pop, rock, and soul music with ease and when released easily became the hugest hit of the band's career. The song peaked as an angelic gospel-sounding choir kicked in, listening the song far and away above the city. And who were these angelic voices? Yes, it was John Frusciante's mother and her friends from the church choir. The song would later famously be watered-down into a R&B/pop reworking by British all-girl quartet All Saints, who enjoyed massive success with their own passable version.

For Flea, this watershed song held a key moment in his remembrance of that album and indeed his feelings towards the Red Hot Chili Peppers: "Myself and John, we were playing 'Under The Bridge', largely live like we did on all that record. Right at the last outro, we both looked each other at the exact same time and did an improvised little fill that could have been any combination of notes at any given time… but we both did the *exact* same thing at the *exact* same time. For me, the magic of that record is distilled into that one little (moment)."

'Under The Bridge' was a hard song to top, so the cumbersome funk of 'Naked In The Rain' paled in comparison. It wasn't the first tune the band had written about the jungle, the animal kingdom and being down with Momma Earth either – although it was first to address a Doctor Doolittle. Similarly 'Apache Rose Peacock' seems like cookie-cutter Chili Peppers, too formulaic to hold its own against the album's strongest moments, although Kiedis' story of sitting on a sack of beans in New Orleans and being blown away by a jaw-droppingly beautiful lady by the name of Apache Rose Peacock is endearing enough.

'The Greeting Song' was a fast, technical song that played on the two guitarist's abilities, although the band appeared to forget to write a discernible chorus. A tender song 'My Lovely Man' is far from maudlin – indeed, it's funky enough and true to the band's original blueprint to make the erstwhile guitarist proud of his bro's. More fine bass work from Flea. Like 'Suck My Kiss' before it – or indeed, anything on the band's first three albums – 'Sir Psycho Sexy' was a flagrantly dumb and seemingly sexist fantasy song. And clocking in at eight minutes, an overly one at that. The particular scenario this time was a character called Sir Psycho Sexy who, amongst other things, makes it with a cop. A lady cop, that is. Shame the song wasn't strong enough to support such a ridiculous lyrical indulgence. Album closer, that appropriately-titled cover version of old-time bluesman Robert Johnson's 'They're Red Hot', was better - a fun roaring rag-time skiffle shuffle that sent listeners on their way with a smile on their face and a wiggle in their stride.

The stunning cover depicted their four heads in profile, tongues intertwined to create a tribal pattern centred around a red rose, the album artwork affirmed the brotherly status of a band who were on the verge of going global. The design included pictures by Gus van Sant, who also directed the 'Under The Bridge' video and with whom Flea worked on the movie *My Own Private Idaho*. Anthony's tattooist friend 'Henky Penky' (his customers call him Mr Henk Schiffmacher!) designed the trademark intertwining tongue design. Schiffmacher works out of the museum of tattooing in Amsterdam, Holland, and first met Anthony during a European jaunt to promote *Freaky Styley*. The son of a butcher who was rejected from the army on grounds of his mental health, has annotated the flesh of several US bands, including the Foo Fighters and Ramones.

Bloodsugarsexmagik was an international phenomenon. The album was released on the same day as the landmark album *Nevermind* by Nirvana, and that was one of the few contemporary releases whose sales could match those of the Chili Peppers. The four words in the title unwittingly represent the four corners of the band, four characteristics at once complimentary and at the same time entirely individual. The concept of blood/life, sex/creative energy and the link between magic and music developed beyond simply the title of one of the tracks to declare itself the natural title for the album. Earning platinum status, it stayed on the *Billboard* chart for over a year. Rubin allowed the band the space to let their more personal feelings and experiences flood into the music. This wasn't an album about how great a bass line or a riff was. The Red Hot Chili Peppers finally had more sensitive things to say, and on this breakthrough album they found the way of saying them that had eluded them previously. In particular "Under The Bridge" found a way of saying some awful things in a beautiful way.

Sex was still something to write about, and Kiedis was happy to admit the fact: "It seems like the perfect material for art," he told David Fricke in 1992. "Like death and every other fundamental aspect of existence... it's right up there with the biggies as far as I can tell." Amused at the thought of a Kansas housewife buying the album for its 'sweet, sentimental songs' only to get it home and have her ears turned inside-out by 'Sir Psycho Sexy,' Kiedis pictured her "washing her dishes in her little home... popping this in and taking off her clothes and getting loosened up a bit."

The amazing year was topped off with a sell-out show at the San Francisco Cow Palace, playing to 14,500 people alongside Nirvana and Pearl Jam. That single show grossed $400,000. The Chilis were now in the big time.

Rick Rubin had brought the best out of the band and Bloodsugarsexmagik is still the most critically-acclaimed Chilis album. When 'Under The Bridge' peaked at number two in the Billboard listing and charted in most countries with a major power supply, the band were simultaneously vindicated, enlivened and inspired. And so began a new era in the curious tale of the Red Hot Chili Peppers...

CHAPTER 11

Tattoos are a big thing with the Chili Peppers. Anthony has an astounding eagle design tattooed on his back that took many, many hours to apply. He has daggers on his forearms and two Indian Chiefs. The armband on Kiedis's right arm is a stylised flower while a broken heart design is added to the matching one on his left arm. A tiger, added in 2001, was to help him get over the pain of breaking up with his girlfriend, and represents both his Chinese birth sign and the Thai tradition of tigers bringing longevity and protection to the wearer – and he enjoys adding the detail that he is Tony the Tiger, the cartoon cat from the Kelloggs Frosties ads.

John has an ornate pink octopus on his arm in honour of the tour that promoted *Mother's Milk*. Like Anthony he bears the asterisk logo of the band on his wrist, and on his left upper arm he too has a Native American Indian design, while a design inspired by an Ornette Coleman album sleeve is on his left forearm. A design on his right wrist can be viewed to reveal a man and a woman in the process of making out.

Chad is relatively clear of tattoos: on his right arm he carries a large scorpion design, while on his left arm he has a stylised eagle design in a kind of heraldic badge. Chinese characters representing the names of Chad's two children are on his inner arms, while – like Frusciante – he has an octopus, but this one lies worryingly on Chad's thigh.

Flea, like Anthony, is a veritable walking gallery of tattoo designs. On his left arm he bears a striking picture of Jimi Hendrix and the name of his daughter, next to a string of coloured elephants that encircle his bicep. Inside his left arm is an abstract design, while on each of his knuckles he has the word 'love.' On his chest Flea has an old Celtic design, symbolising birth, death and eternity, while opposite – like a little logo – he carries the name of his ex-wife Loesha. Birds decorate the inside of Flea's right arm, but more visible is a fabulous concoction in which a snake was added to a pair of dolphins and a celtic dragon. On his back Flea has another tribal design stretching from shoulder blade to shoulder blade.

Anthony speaks of his tattoos like battle scars or campaign medals. "It's beautiful to watch them grow old and fade," he says. "They're all representative of times in my life." He bears two Maori designs on his forearms, and on his right wrist the chunky asterisk that acts as the Peppers' logo.

The band sold out *every single gig* on the world tour that supported *Bloodsugarsexmagik*, and made the front pages of magazines the world over. This was their breakthrough moment – comparable to the moments when U2, Eminem, Madonna and countless other household names move from cult status to ubiquity. As so often, in retrospect it should have been clear to anyone with an ear and an eye for a great live band that *Mother's Milk* was going to be followed by something spectacular, but few could have predicted the explosive increase in interest in the band who were – after all – eight years into their career.

'Give It Away,' the single release, was one of the sharpest records in the collection, winning excessive airplay and an MTV award for 'Best Breakthrough Video'. "We knew it was a watershed," said Kiedis. French director Stephane Sednaoui took the band out to the desert for the video, a classy black and white clip featuring gallons of silver body paint, sprayed Dr Martens boots, a barrel full of surrealistic horns and cool silver mirror pants. Sednaoui's focus on the band's 'performance' in front of camera was so intense that there is an almost orgiastic abandon to the video, as the band rock out before turning away to disappear into the rapidly setting silver sunset. Possibly the very first Chilis video that you watched and then said, "I gotta see that band play live!"

Rock historians often cite 1991 as the year that Nirvana, Pearl Jam and the other Seattle-led punk bands broke out and began to challenge the permed stranglehold that Guns N' Roses and Metallica had over rock. In fact they did so supporting The Red Hot Chili Peppers, and it was *Bloodsugarsexmagik* that signalled more than any other that the days of the strutting peacocks of glam metal were over at last.

Yet it is grunge, not the Chili's funk-punk, that the start of the Nineties is renowned for. At the start of that decade, the new music phenomenon christened grunge spread across the globe the revolutionised the world of music and youth fashion. Its epicentre was on the north-western seaboard of the USA, in Seattle Washington. Prior to the Nineties, Seattle was not famed for its alternative music. Of course, it could claim Jimi Hendrix amongst its forefathers, and there were other successes such as the Sonics, the Fleetwoods, and several more mainstream artists such as Robert Cray, Heart, Kenny G, Quincy Jones and Queensryche. However, these highpoints were sporadic and isolated, with no thread of association between the respective artists.

RED HOT CHILI PEPPERS

As the Eighties headed towards a climax, an underground scene – just like that which had spewed forth the Chilis – was developing that would, during a brief flurry of breath-taking musical brilliance, turn the global mainstream on its head. Grunge's backdrop was the sweeping recessions that were suffocating the economies of the western world in the early Nineties. America suffered as much as any country and with predictable social results – alienation, poverty and rebellion. Although grunge was absolutely a US-born movement, it found thousands of welcoming fans in the UK, where the recession was similarly disenchanting millions. Countless homeowners were deep in negative equity, unemployment queues were lengthening and dissatisfaction with Tory rule growing. The student population was rife with anger at educational fees and sweeping reforms of the NHS and other nationalised institutions. All this made the UK and other countries throughout Europe a place of indifference and pessimism, and a terrain where grunge could take a hold.

Starting in that cold, northwestern corner of the United States, grunge began life as a disparate group of bands gigging relentlessly on the underground circuit, with no real eye for the ensuing avalanche of multi-platinum record sales and sold-out world tours. The record label Sub Pop is seen by many as at the very nucleus of this era of music, releasing a seminal series of limited edition records, in the process airing classic tracks by bands such as Sonic Youth, Steve Fisk, the U-Men, Skinny Puppy, Nirvana, and the often overlooked Green River.

Aside from these names, there were hordes of other bands producing alternative music of note in this period. The quite brilliant Tad, Mudhoney, the Screaming Trees - these and many others released music that, to the youth of the day at least, was revolutionary. Bands like the Melvins and Sonic Youth also enjoyed rejuvenated careers in the wake of numerous citations from the younger bands they had influenced. Older detractors derided grunge's fusion of hardcore and metal as merely re-hashing Seventies rock, but this mattered little to those who were experiencing such music for the first time. It felt like they were living through something important. Besides, the scuzzy, furious raw energy of grunge was rooted much more in the post-punk barrage of US hardcore bands like Black Flag (who were themselves compared to bands like Led Zeppelin). Also, there was a clear lineage back to Sixties garage bands like the Sonics, MC5, the Stooges and the Kingsmen.

Like all subcultures and musical movements, this latest development was only tagged after it had already been around for some time (indeed, the term grunge itself was originally a tongue-in-cheek name). By then Nirvana had gone global with their ten million-selling *Nevermind* album, which single-handedly changed the face of modern music programming, live shows, record store buying policies and just about every facet of the music and entertainment industries. For example, in the wake of 'Smells Like Teen Spirit', MTV's aesthetic was virtually transformed overnight, ditching the bikini-clad babes of a thousand soft porn metal videos and replacing them with grunge's more gritty, cheaper look. For the next two years, grunge ruled the world. By the time Kurt Cobain killed himself in April, 1994, the movement had already lost its essence anyway, diluted by a corporate-hijacking and mainstream acceptance.

It's not clear exactly how the Red Hot Chili Peppers fitted into all this. Their songs and sound was as far from many of grunge's highlights as could be imagined – take Pearl Jam's massive hit 'Jeremy' for example with its themes of teenage suicide and personal despair, compared to 'Suck My Kiss'. The Chilis were party animals, whereas most grungers were (on the surface at least) dour, troubled introverts. Visually there were some similarities, and many of grunge's acolytes shared billing with the Chilis around the globe's festival circuit. But other than that, the Chili Peppers seemed largely at odds with the prevailing mood and musical fashion of the time. But the record company couldn't get copies of *Bloodsugarsexmagik* into the shops quick enough. Odd but true, they were the outsiders who were the headliners. What's more, they had years of experience ahead of their grunge counterparts with which to cope with the obstacles of fame (or so it seemed).

No longer kids, the band (Frusciante apart) were all pushing thirty years of age, their cock-rock days rapidly disappearing into the past, and their more reflective, adult audience mirrored in their own songwriting. Frusciante even revealed that he spent more time playing the clarinet than the guitar off-stage. While John threatened to turn into a woodwind player on tour, Flea carried his trumpet – that he had been playing since age eleven – with him too.

Anthony's focus was better than ever. Clean since Hillel's death, his late friend still reminded him every day of who was underneath the rock-icon front that the public saw. In the late spring of 1992, Anthony received a package in the mail from a friend, containing a brown paper box that Hillel had given Kiedis back in 1986. On the box was an inscription from Slovak to his band-mate and friend: "Anthony. You think what I feel and understand what I say. I love you. This is our year." In March, Anthony became a brother again (he already had two sisters) – well, a step-brother – when young James Kiedis, twenty nine years younger than his brother was born. As he grew up, James could occasionally be seen with Anthony on stage, as, during the 'One Hot Minute' tour, he sang backing vocals with Rain Phoenix. Rain was the sister of the equally wonderfully-named River, with whom she had sung and performed from the age of three. Together with Johnny Depp and her late brother, she has had a long and friendly relationship with the band, and has appeared in a handful of movies too, most notably in *Even Cowgirls Get The Blues*.

'Under The Bridge', was a natural for FM radio (the American record industry likes nothing more than songs about American cities and Anthony knew it was a potential hit when a drunk guy at a party stood next to him at the urinal and belted the song out while he took a piss. Its success was bolstered by a very poignant video that slowed the pace of the Chilis down for the public for the very first time, visually as well as musically. Gus van Sant directed the superb clip, combining beautifullyshot images of the band in monochrome yellows, oranges and purples, with footage of Anthony walking the streets of his beloved LA. As Anthony raps with passers-by, John plays guitar in a trippy, green woolly hat, Flea plays bass literally under a bridge, and Anthony himself wears a fitting 'To Hell & Back' T-shirt. As the video comes to a close, Anthony escapes down the LA river, as the mushroom cloud of an atomic explosion destroys the city behind him.

Bloodsugarsexmagik was also the band's first truly international album. It was huge *everywhere*. Shows in 1992 in London, at the Brixton Academy, were well-received, and despite being refused a spot on *Top of the Pops*, the all-important UK market was clearly coming around. This was a heady time for bands like the Chili Peppers: 'new' on the circuit with a blistering live set and a fabulous album to promote. Back in the States they shared bills with Nirvana, Pearl Jam and The Smashing Pumpkins, all themselves riding the crest of the rock new wave. The Australian and

Asian markets started to wake up to the band – they could do no wrong. Critically too this was high water for the band: critics and airheads alike began to realise that this was not a band solely obsessed with waving sock-covered dicks around or with having a rock and roll good time. It was clear that this was a band born out of Miles Davis as much as Funkadelic, equally the offspring of Hendrix and Black Flag, with a growing social conscience and an interest in broader affairs than just sex, drugs and rock and roll.

Always the most in-demand musically, Flea recorded sessions for 'It's A Miracle', a track on former Pink Floyd leader Roger Waters' solo album *Amused To Death*, which was released in September. Because of touring commitments he was forced to decline the offer to work on a new album by Jeff Beck, the lost guitar hero of the Sixties and Seventies.

When the band finished touring *Bloodsugarsexmagik* in Australia and New Zealand, most of the band returned to LA. Anthony – a long-time lover of exploration trips and hiking, took off to Borneo with Henky Penky, the tattooist befriended by the band. Henk Schiffmacher and Anthony Kiedis nearly became 'The Lost Men Of Borneo', their trek beset by dengue fever, diarrhoea, dysentery and puking sessions, being totally disorientated and fighting off ravenous leeches. Penky wrote a Dutch-language book, *De Grote Borneo Expeditie*, about the affair, a great adventure for both men that started on Borneo's west coast and became what Kiedis described to *Rolling Stone* as a "Vietnam experience". Over-run by mosquitoes, with bugs the size of Volkswagens climbing in and out of their ears, wet, uncomfortable and a long way from home, Kiedis told the magazine that "when you're a white guy from California, and you've run out of food, and you can't fluidly communicate with your guides, it becomes a source of concern."

The trip through Borneo was a gamble for Kiedis, and a gimmick in that theme marked the band's 'goodbye gig' for 1992 at the Hard Rock Hotel in Las Vegas in kind. The band had casino chips designed for the evening: a $5 band chip, a $100 band chip, and individual chips for the four members of the band at $25 each.

In 1992, the Chili Peppers won their first ever Grammy award, for the 'Best Hard Rock Performance With Vocal,' at the 35th award ceremony. 'Give It Away', from *Bloodsugarsexmagic* was the winning song. They also co-presented at the same year's MTV Award ceremony with the cool-again singer Tony Bennett. Bennett described Flea as being like a young Jimmy Durante, an old time actor-cum-singer, "very mischievous and spontaneous." Bennett won over the MTV audience with a catchy quote from their Grammy winning song, and from that moment on found a whole raft of young people suddenly attending his concerts. The following year – February 1993 – the Chilis would later play with the P Funk All Stars at the Grammy awards at LA's Shrine auditorium.

That same year, EMI released *What Hits!?* Apparently a celebration of their journey so far, it was in fact a hastily compiled selection of tracks intended to get the most out of the success of *Bloodsugarsexmagik*. A video of much the same material was put together too, and was perhaps slightly more interesting in that it featured Frusciante and Smith on 'Behind The Sun,' where of course it had been Slovak and Irons playing on the original track. The video also included live footage of the band in their sock outfits ('Jungle Man'), and artwork by Robert Williams, the creator of the controversial artwork on Guns N' Roses' *Appetite For Destruction*. The video was a worthy companion to a collection of Chili Pepper albums, neatly summarising their work up to 'Under The Bridge'. If these bits of Chili Peppers re-packaging were a slice of cynical commercialism, the series of ads that Anthony appeared in for GAP were a trifle more artistic in their conception. Photographer Annie Liebowitz caught Anthony at his handsome, most muscular best, his long hair almost to his waist.

With album sales already exceeding one million for *Bloodsugarsexmagik* alone, and with the back catalogue resurfacing in the sales print-outs of record stores everywhere, the Chili Peppers were booked to headline the highly prestigious 1992 Lollapalooza 2 tour, appearing above acts such as Ice Cube, Ministry, Pearl Jam and Soundgarden. By May they were in the Far East, opening a lengthy tour schedule in Japan. Only days into the Japanese leg of the tour, May 7th 1992, John Frusciante quit the Red Hot Chili Peppers... The end came initially at the first of these Japanese shows. Lindy Goetz, the band's manager called in to the venue to check that preparations for the evening's show were going to plan only to be told that John had left the band. He and the rest of the Chilis managed to persuade John not to leave and eventually the guitarist did perform that night. But the very next morning, he quit, as far as he was concerned at that moment, for good. Frusciante returned to the United States the following morning.

There were about three weeks to go before Lollapalooza. The man many credited with revitalising the band and pulling it back from the brink had gone.

CHAPTER 12

The stories about why John Frusciante quit The Red Hot Chili Peppers are legion. In short, he had joined the band too young, joined the heady lifestyle of a headline touring rock band at an age when he ought to have been working his way through his first high-school bands. The pressures and the temptations were too great, and they began to have serious effects on John's psyche. It was almost inevitable that he would crack. "I had a weird premonition that I should quit immediately after I finished my guitar parts on *Bloodsugarsexmagik*," he told *RAW* magazine. He didn't, because he felt simply that the band wouldn't let him go. Too entrenched in their lifestyle and with so much staked on the future of the album and the band, he carried on. Instinct told him that a life continuously on the road might destroy him, and he watched at first hand the effect that the life was having on other members of the band. Relationships between him and Anthony weren't good – in fact at times it was rumoured they were barely talking, and they hardly looked at one another when they were on stage. "Me and Anthony basically toured together for a year without talking at all and things got worse and worse." He had told Flea that there was nothing he liked about being in the band – other than, of course, his love for the guys in it, and the love of playing the guitar. Time marched on, and nothing was done about the situation until it reached an almighty impasse for John. It showed: "John was up there like he didn't give a fuck about anything," said Chad on VH-1, "but you can't be in a group and not care. It is going to show and it did – a lot of the shows were terrible."

Frusciante hated being popular. He hated the adulation and the fame. Fan stories which other band would swoon over were anathema to his very essence, his motivation to play music. One anecdote tells how two groupie-wannabes managed to get into the Chili Peppers' dressing room after a show but the band had already left. Only their tour manager was there wrapping up the night's work. They squealed at him and asked if the band had left any momentoes behind – he duly pointed out that a pair of Flea's famous, large white cotton Y-front underpants were in the corner on the (less than spotless) floor. To the tour manager's amazement, the two girls rushed to the pants, and the lucky winner grabbed them screaming, before raising them above her mouth and wringing out a bead of dirty sweat into her throat. "Now I have a piece of him in me forever," she is said to have sighed. Now for most rock stars and fans of rock music, this was merely a humorous albeit weird tour tale. To someone like John

Frusciante, this was a hideous embodiment of the grotesque monster that was fame. He couldn't bear it.

One of the reasons John had joined the band in the first place was his love of the Chili Peppers as they were when he first saw them. He never envisaged a time when they would play major tours and stadiums around the world, never mind gigs beyond the theatres and clubs of LA. He remembered Hillel, back in the days when he was a fan of the band rather than a member of it, asking John if he would still love the band "if they got so popular they played the LA Forum." Back then his answer was "no" – he couldn't imagine that he could love the band if it escaped from the local scene that he loved so much. By the time the band hit the Japanese gigs where he quit, and with the Lollapalooza dates looming, he simply couldn't tolerate it any longer.

Later, John was to look back at his troubled early years with the band and conclude that he was too young to cope, but also that he was responsible for neglecting himself and his responsibilities. "When I see pictures of myself back then I just want to strangle (that) person," he told *The Guardian* newspaper. "I think that when I was a young, confused and stupid person who actually hadn't lived much, I think I really wanted to be who I am now."

Frusciante's leaving should by rights have killed this band off. Few groups survive intact after so many tragedies and losses. There would be more down the road of course, but at this point they were nearly ten years in the business, and anyone could have forgiven Flea and Anthony for throwing in the towel. Maybe the Chili Peppers would splinter into a handful of new projects? Maybe they would retire from the scene entirely? Frusciante left the band in a creative desert, lost to the colder wasteland of heroin, yet his leaving was not acrimonious. If John wanted smaller gigs, more personal music, wanted out of the big-time rock life and to take a step back into smaller bands and one-off gigs, then ultimately his friends would support him. Anthony later talked of how he too thought Frusciante was simply too young to take the attention, tired of people 'throwing themselves at him.' Tired of TV interviewers and tired of record company responsibilities, John was clearly out of step with the requirements of being a rock hero. At eighteen, he said, he was totally abusing the situation. Japanese and Australasian gigs were cancelled. Kiedis was stunned: "I could tell by the look in his eye that he was really serious," he told journalist David Fricke. There had been tension on the road, low morale, but it was the combined pressures of joining this hard-living group of people and going from playing along to their records to leading their onslaught on the worldwide stage that got to John.

Once he was over the initial shock, Kiedis managed to remain philosophical. "It's bad timing," he was quoted as saying at the time, "but we've always managed to persevere... I think we're going to hook up with somebody that burns and smokes and does what needs to be done."

Kiedis is rumoured to have really struggled with his own demons after John left the band. A recovering addict who had managed to dump his own heroin habit, the last thing he needed was to see John slide into an addiction of his own, particularly given the history of Hillel. But although Anthony has managed to clean up for good, it is never an easy ride for a former addict when surrounded by other users.

Leaving aside Frusciante's escalating terrors with heroin addiction for the time being, the band still needed a new guitar player, and they needed him fast. They found Arik Marshall, an LA guitarist playing with his brother in Marshall Law, veterans of the local funk scene in Los Angeles. Lonnie Law, Arik's brother, went on to form a new band, Weapon of Choice, who released critically acclaimed albums such as *Nutmeg Sez 'Bozo The Town'* and *Hyperspice*. Arik told the press that he had "figured that these guys were gonna check me out." He walked and talked it like a Chili Pepper from day one.

Arik had less than three weeks to learn the Chili Peppers' set before he endured a literal baptism of fire, playing his first gig with the band in front of 60,000 fans at San Francisco's Shoreline Amphitheatre. He rehearsed for five hours a day in preparation, learning Hillel Slovak's and John Frusciante's parts frantically. The 'baptism of fire' was that he had to wear the costume designed for the band: flame-throwing helmets that spewed out flames above the heads of the band members as they careered around the stage. Health and Safety officials would have had a field day if they had been able to carry out risk assessments on the band, but the risks for Arik went beyond simply setting light to himself. The helmets frightened the life out of the new guitarist, and in a sense they calmed his nerves about the size of the gig he was about to play. By the time he had come to terms with playing his guitar with his head on fire, he was settled into the concert and carried the whole thing off with considerable aplomb.

Marshall seemed a worthy replacement for Frusciante, yet it was not to be. Flea, Kiedis, and to a lesser extent Smith, were a hard act to please – not in the sense of playing ability, but to be in this band you had to be in their family. The Chili Peppers have always been big on love: they are a band of personalities that gel before they are a band of musicians who gel, and somehow Arik just didn't fit.

While the band's own dates to support *Bloodsugarsexmagik* were a significant step up in profile, it was perhaps their showing at the 34-date 1992 Lollapalooza tour that brought them to an even higher profile. The brainchild of Jane's Addiction's Perry Farrell, Lollapalooza re-invented the festival for a modern era with a myriad of musical styles accompanied by information about a variety of important issues. At each stadium-sized show there would be stalls organised by major and minor protest groups, such as Greenpeace, gun control lobbyists and civil liberties groups. Tattooists and fire-eaters added to the general Bohemian atmosphere and the resultant tour package was a phenomenal success - in many senses this was in fact the real follow up to Woodstock.

Arik lasted out the Lollapalooza 2 tour, which was a huge success both as a tour for all who were on it and for the Chili Peppers themselves. On a personal note, Flea recalled this as a great time, despite John's recent departure, because "we had a blast, there was no tension, we went out and had a lot of fun." In addition, with 'Under The Bridge' continuing to build up a wave of support since its spring release, the band were receiving adulation like they had never had it before. Unfortunately Arik didn't last much longer. Although he had the chops to make it as a guitarist in the band, his personality was simply not right for the rest of the band, and everyone knew it. Despite the short length of time he had to learn their catalogue and get to know them properly, Arik was a red-hot live guitarist on the Lollapalooza tour, but his time in the harsh glare of the Chili's limelight was over, returning ultimately to his brother's band Weapon of Choice.

Next up the band placed an ad in the LA press advertising for yet another replacement. An astounding *five thousand* applicants responded, and out of them emerged Mother's Tongue guitarist Jesse Tobias. Despite looking just right for the band, two months later Tobias was out too: constantly searching for a new Hillel Slovak, the band found it hard to come to terms with the fact that no such guitarist was out there. Tobias went on to tour with Alanis Morissette, fell in love with a member of her support act, and moved to Australia, where he married and still resides.

If a new guitarist was to successfully join the Peppers, then Kiedis and crew would have to find someone with his (or her) own personality, someone unique and capable of bringing the band into line with their own style as much as joining in with theirs. In John Frusciante they had found their man. Sadly, in them, he found his own route to the doors of death. Four years dead, Slovak was still an impossible act to follow amongst this remarkable group of people.

Beating has-beens, newcomers and legends including U2, Clapton and Queen to the honours, The Red Hot Chili Peppers came home from the 1992 MTV awards with three awards from eight nominations. Funk – a displaced, increasingly minority backwater of black American dance music – had been dragged kicking and screaming back into the full glare of the pop spotlight. Flea, however, was not able to enjoy the party for too much longer.

Increasingly exhausted by the endless touring regime and the pressures of being in a world-profile band, Flea's constitution had lasted longer than that of any other member of the band. Hillel had paid the ultimate price. Kiedis was a victim of the same excesses, and had developed problems of his own. Frusciante had quit in order to keep himself sane, and Jack Irons had barely survived the same problems. Neither Peligro, Marshall or Jesse Tobias had lasted too long either for different reasons. Flea, however, had what it took by the truck-load, but eventually, even for him, the strain was too much. "I couldn't eat, I couldn't sleep, and as soon as the tour was over I let my body relax for a moment and I just crashed," was how Flea described it.

In 1993, Flea was diagnosed with chronic fatigue syndrome, a debilitating state of total exhaustion. On stage at the Viper Room on October 30th, - where he would jam with friends such as actor Johnny Depp (who co-owned the Viper Room) - he watched as close friend River Phoenix was helped outside by friends. Despite the efforts of paramedics who were quickly on the scene, the violent seizures suffered by Phoenix outside The Viper Room were his final moments, and his death added to Flea's illness (Flea went in the ambulance with River). River Phoenix was pronounced dead on October 31st. It was the day before Anthony's thirtieth birthday. Kiedis was in New York City. He cried for twenty four hours when he heard the news. Flea was ordered to rest not for one week, not for a month but for a *year* by his doctor. Perhaps this was time for the Red Hot Chili Peppers to call it a day?

CHAPTER 13

The history of the Red Hot Chilli Peppers is, however, one of remarkable survival. Where they could have given in to the pressures that brought on Flea's illness, instead they soldiered on. Cancelled gigs and personal schedules that allowed a glimpse of normality meant, in fact, that this was an ideal time to scratch around for that new guitar player. In ex-Jane's Addiction and Deconstruction guitarist Dave Navarro, they finally believed they had found the man capable of filling Slovak and Frusciante's lofty shoes.

David Michael Navarro was born on June 7th, 1967 in Santa Monica, California, the son of a Spanish immigrant father and American mother. Dave began his musical career early, starting to play the piano at the age of six, and moving to a second-hand acoustic guitar around the age of eleven. His parents divorced when he was seven-years-old, and using cannabis from the age of eleven, he felt disengaged from his parents from an early age. Upon hearing Jimi Hendrix, his conversion on the road to the rock and roll Damascus came at a skateboard park, and from that moment on he knew what business he wanted to be in. Navarro was influenced by many styles of guitar-playing, but after a metal period he was in particular drawn to English bands like The Cure and Bauhaus, distinctive outfits whose guitar strength relied not so much on technique – although under the influence of Eddie van Halen, Dave himself had developed excellent technique – but on sound quality and the nature of the noises created by the instrument.

Dave suffered a shocking experience when, at the age of fifteen, his mother and aunt was brutally murdered by his mother's boyfriend, a man who Dave had loved like family. Dave was out of the house, but the man broke in and shot the sisters dead. "It's kind of a powerful message to send to an evolving mind," he said with massive understatement in 1995. Already traumatised by his parent's divorce (he recounted how he sat in front of mirrors pulling the taste buds from his tongue and to have cut himself with razor blades as a child), this dreadfully painful experience cut Navarro in two: "I had a lot of stuff bottled up inside me, and the only way I could get it out was if I sat in my room and played the guitar." The murderer was not caught until TV show *America's Most Wanted* turned him up in 1996 – Dave became a key witness in his prosecution.

Navarro was also becoming involved in soft drugs. He went to live with his father, and, dismissed from school in the 11th grade for poor achievement and he could potentially have ended up in deep trouble. Through friends and contacts in his first tentative band, Navarro met the three guys who would catapult him into the spotlight for the first time.

Jane's Addiction, the influential art-rock quartet from Los Angeles, were formed in 1986 by Perry Farrell on the back of the demise of his first band Psi Com. With Navarro on guitar, Eric Avery on bass and Stephen Perkins on drums, they released their eponymous first album – a live affair – in 1987. Mixing up punk rock, folk, funk and every influence from Lou Reed to PiL, they were a fascinating band: intelligent rhythms; disjointed, artful guitar; intense vocals. Jane's Addiction never quite matched in achievements what they offered in potential. Studio sessions would be cancelled due to in-house fights; drugs became a major source of friction. Flea played trumpet on 'Idiots Rule', from the album *Nothing's Shocking*. Interviewed after he joined the Chili Peppers, Dave remembered Perry Farrell showing Flea what to play, and they spoke of how this gradually turned into a 'playing together' thing.

By 1990 the cracks were more than evident, despite a growing fan base, and when Farrell launched the concept of the travelling-circus music festival called Lollapalooza, it became clear that his band had insurmountable problems. Navarro announced that he would quit the band at the end of the tour. Fist-fights with Perry as they waited to take the stage; stage gear thrown into the audience in anger: this was clearly an unhappy band. After the last show of the tour, on September 27th 1991, the four band members parted, but not before Navarro and Flea formed a strong friendship.

With bass player Eric Avery, Navarro formed a new project called Deconstruction, but this lasted for one album, released in 1994. Although he had initially been approached by the Chili Peppers on the departure of John Frusciante, Navarro had declined, as Deconstruction was taking up all his attentions at the time. He also had bad vibes about extensive touring post-Lollapalooza, and didn't want the kind of schedule that the famously hard-touring Chili Peppers were planning. Thirdly, Deconstruction was a creative process in which he was enjoying flexing his song-writing muscles, and to have joined the Peppers at this time would have been to have gone out playing someone else's old material. Navarro had known the band since the mid-Eighties, playing the same gigs and hanging around in the same party scene around LA. Wooed by Guns N'Roses as well as by the Chili Peppers (in 1999 he played on Guns N'Roses' 'Oh My God', featured in the movie *End Of Days*), Navarro was in a strong position. "He'd build me up and say 'There's no other guitarist in the world capable of filling that role except me,'" Kiedis told the press. "…and then go, 'Sorry, I can't do it.'" Where Anthony began to lose patience, Chad Smith – disenchanted by the number of crap players he had auditioned since Marshall's leaving – persevered.

By September 1993, the time was right, and Dave Navarro became the new guitar player in the Red Hot Chili Peppers on a permanent basis. Fresh from an unhappy divorce (he had been married in 'a pagan ceremony'), carrying with him personal and narcotic baggage enough to weigh down many another men, Navarro was a perfect addition to this memorably dysfunctional crew of musicians. Visitors to his home noted its 'Addams Family' style: the walls covered in dark, heavy velvet; ouija boards, skulls and a statue of Pan on a shelf in the living room, next to a silver crucifix; a coffin set up as a coffee table; Warhol's 'Electric Chair' and Francis Bacon's screaming pope prints on the wall; a skeleton languorously draped over a sofa. "It's not real," he told Ann Magnuson for *Spin* magazine: "I won't have a real human head in the house!" This was a man with (a certain kind of) style!

Magnuson found Dave in entertaining mood: he showed her around his house, pointing out the collection of vinyl and rubber clothing, an impressive array of T-shirts in varying shades of black, and a pair of black patent-leather size 12 pumps. This dark side would become evident in the band's visual presentation: the video for the single 'Warped' featured an S&M-designed, homo-erotic session between Anthony and Dave, which Dave dismissed with a flourish. "Perry Farrell and I used to kiss all the time…" "One guy at Warner Bros. told us to stop making pretentious, faggy videos!" added Flea. "I thought I looked really suave!" Flea has spoken of the feminine element that Dave brought into the band, an element that – on top of the fact that these were guys with a history of taking their kit off in public – endeared them to the gay community as much as to the straight. "That's great for me. I love that," said Flea. "I can be a fag!"

Dave is a pure musician through and through – his first paying job at age fifteen was playing at the Troubadour in Los Angeles, and he proudly boasts of never having had to queue in line for the usual crappy jobs in fast-food joints and gas stations. Navarro brought real potential back into the band, but it was a confused band that he joined. "We were like Spinal Tap", recalled Chad Smith for *Rolling Stone*, "but it was the guitar player that kept exploding."

From the very beginning, although Navarro made a special contribution to the Red Hot Chili Peppers, and probably saved them at a time when they would have died otherwise, it ought to have been clear that this arrangement wouldn't last forever. "The truth is," said Dave, "I'm not much of a funk fan. I'm more into dark music." Although Dave expected them to be wacky, funky and cute, he found the band apparently open to his influences and happy to bring him on board as an element of change. "We wanted to make something new together," said Anthony. They certainly did that.

In true showbiz style, Dave made his Chili Pepper debut dressed as a giant light bulb. His first major public appearance was in front of a quarter of a million people at Woodstock II, on August 14th 1994. The bill included Dylan, Nine Inch Nails, Cypress Hill, The Rollins Band, Porno for Pyros and more. Dave made no secret of the fact that he wasn't entirely in agreement with the band's costume idea, but went along with it nonetheless. Fortunately, it turned around for him as the light bulb costume helped Dave – like Arik before him – overcome his nerves for that first show. Although it was stinking hot, uncomfortable and restricted his ability to play, those very things meant that the only thing he could do was to concentrate on trying to play his instrument, and he forgot about the crowd. "I hadn't performed in front of an audience that size in years," he told *Alternative Press* magazine. "By the time I emerged from (it), my fear had subsided."

Two weeks later, and the light bulb costumes had travelled with the band to the UK for the Reading festival, Dave's first date in the UK for the Chili Peppers. This was the first time that the guys had played in Britain since 1992, and their new member received a mighty welcome. The band still had that love-hate relationship with the UK. "To be perfectly honest," Anthony told *Kerrang!*, England is not our favourite place to go." Some might have thought this was some reaction to record sales, or maybe the band didn't get the live reception they enjoyed elsewhere? No: "It's the weather we don't like," said Kiedis. "And it's very far away. And the food is not very good… steak and kidney pie is not really my favourite!"

Settling into the live atmosphere around the band, their juggernaut onslaught on audiences large and small, Navarro brought a lyrical element to the Peppers' percussive, angular funk. His sense of the melodic and what he called the 'ethereal' nature of his playing added to the soup that was their sound. This was, nevertheless, an odd marriage. Not only was he not much of a punk fan, he didn't even have any Chili Peppers albums in his collection. Both parties made it clear that Navarro would not simply drop into an existing format for the guitar slot in the band. "We wanted to make something new together," said Kiedis, and while Dave told the press that he "tiptoed" for the first couple of weeks, it was clear that his joining the band was as much on his terms as theirs. It was far from plain sailing. Still suffering from the emotional and physical stress of Chronic Fatigue Syndrome, Flea found it hard to assimilate the new member. Twice during rehearsals the bass player walked out on the band. Twice he came back and apologised. Still sick, his natural defences down, Flea was unable to get out of bed half the time, and he found the concept of a new guitarist in his band hard to handle. The battle to keep the Chili Peppers alive was still far from over.

CHAPTER 14

In the new year of 1994, the Red Hot Chili Peppers headed out for Hawaii. Sun, sea and surf would put them in a better frame of mind, bring them together instead of let them drift further apart. They rode horses, surfed, swam and went scuba diving: they bonded. The previous world tour had left them mentally and physically exhausted and they were still feeling the effects when they entered the studio to make their first album with Dave Navarro. Relationships were still a little strained, but the break they had had was so rejuvenating that they opted not to return to Rick Rubin's Hollywood Hills mansion, instead staying on in Hawaii for three months to piece together ideas for an album.

If they were to continue to be creative they needed to regenerate their efforts and prepare for the next, perhaps most crucial album. With Navarro still the new boy, and with Flea only gradually getting his self together following illness, Kiedis was having problems on lyrics and melodies. Although he never stopped working, he found the creative muse had temporarily left him. And it was unhelpfully rumoured that heroin had claimed him back. While issuing a categorical denial, Anthony made reference to having survived a huge "personal catastrophic tragedy." Rick Rubin was back on the soundboard, and three months in the sun promised at least the chance of knitting the band back together. They were stressed and emotionally fragile, but they were working together.

Flea took on more of the writing duties than previously, penning substantial sections of the lyrics on new tracks such as 'Deep Kick' and 'Transcending,' while fewer songs grew out of the previously preferred Chili Pepper modus operandi of extended jamming sessions. Developing his guitar technique on a Martin acoustic given to him by Rubin, Flea got himself a Neil Young songbook and simply started to explore chord progressions and song structure. Songs would then develop from his own discoveries, to which Navarro would contribute, or he would come up with a bass line and Dave would wind a guitar part into it. What Flea he found out most of all in the process was that good songs do not come out of song-writing knowledge or technical know-how, but out of the writer being in touch with his self and with his emotions. Out of that comes the song.

While Flea found new depths to his musical self in the making of the next album, Kiedis described the process of making what would come to be called *One Hot Minute* as "a tragic and miraculous struggle of love."

RED HOT CHILI PEPPERS

Although the musical tracks went down pretty quickly, it took Kiedis up to a year to complete his lyrics and vocal contribution. If the band struggled, it was only a part of the greater struggle that seemed to encapsulate their career to date, and it was this lengthy journey that brought the best out of them at the time. Flea was intent on becoming a better songwriter, letting writing take over from bass-playing as his primary concern. His playing here was even more sparse than on *Bloodsugarsexmagic* letting the spaces in the music speak for themselves instead of trying to fill every beat with a note or five. He told *Bass Player* that he had spent more time before recording simply strumming an acoustic guitar than playing his bass, and he felt he had perhaps put up a better performance as a result. Keeping it simple had made it more real.

The album was darker in tone than before, its long gestation frustrating the new guitarist, who sardonically described the endless piecing together as "pretty fucking hilarious." The funk element of the band was less evident than previously, Navarro's guitar sounding rockier than before, muted and edgy. This was clearly a band looking to re-define itself. Navarro's tight, nervy playing brought a different colour to many of the tracks, and the band threw experimental and metal, introspection and psychedelia into the melting pot.

One Hot Minute was released on September 12th, 1995, after a whole bunch of alternative titles had been dismissed (working titles that were later rejected give an insight into the band's state of mind during recordings: *Hypersensitive*, *The Good And Bad Moods Of The Red Hot Chili Peppers* and *The Blight Album*). It was in theory a year late, and although the rest of the band didn't seem particularly worried about it, Navarro still wasn't happy, telling reporters that he felt he could have done better.

Was the little red headed girl playing the piano on the cover some kind of veiled reference to Tori Amos? On Amos' album *Under The Pink*, the track 'Cloud On My Tongue' is rumoured to be about Kiedis, who had allegedly asked Amos to go to Borneo with him. The two certainly had a friendship of sorts – but Tori was reticent about the details when she spoke to a journalist about their supposed affair: "it was an interesting-embarrassing moment," was almost as much as she would admit to. "He's just somebody that you could run away with. He's that kind of person. But, you know – he'd run away with ten million women, and I'm not a habit, I'm a lifestyle, so… it can never happen,"

Unfortunately, despite highlights, the new album was far from the killer comeback it had been talked up to be. *One Hot Minute* was certainly a musically and emotionally diverse affair, again largely due in part to the line-up change. While the Chilis always purveyed a sense of goofy irreverence and boyish tomfoolery, Navarro was cool, aloof, charismatically pessimistic and slightly removed. The band had rightly agreed that rather than fight against their contrasting personalities, they should instead let it inform the new music they were writing. Unfortunately, the net result was a record that met with a lukewarm response and flagging sales – around a million copies in the US, a shuddering *tenth* of their previous album's sales. It wasn't difficult to see why.

A darker offering than their usual album openers, 'Warped' set the tone of what was to come. Both Kurt Cobain and Flea's friend River Phoenix had passed away during the lead-up to *One Hot Minute* and a sudden sense of mortality was buried within the music. Here Kiedis sings over a swirling, heady mix of sound that certainly owes something to the dark psychedelics of Jane's Addiction. It was a far cry from the uplifting *thunk* of previous album openers like 'Fight Like A Brave'; signs perhaps that the good time boys weren't having such a good time.

One of the album's singles, 'Aeroplane' was a stronger song and much more uplifting with a joyous children's choir (including Flea's daughter Clara Balzary) providing the chorus, although the simplistic pop melody did border on the unnecessarily cheesy. It sounded like the Chilis on autopilot, digging deep for a single to sell to MTV.

With a long atmospheric spoken word intro, 'Deep Kick' charted the band's journey from Kiedis and Flea's days at Fairfax High to running free in the dirty city and into what they had become. Reminiscent of Jim Morrison, Kiedis delivered a powerful, affecting speech before the song exploded into standard high-energy funk rock that sounds like a precursor to a later hit, 'Can't Stop'. By its conclusion, it had turned into something else – a bluesy outro with laconic vocals by an off-kilter but beautiful sounding Flea. 'My Friends', a downbeat hindsight song about brotherhood and love and another single release, was vaguely reminiscent of 'Under The Bridge', their biggest hit to date – harshly judged by some critics as an attempt to cling to the new-found mainstream record-buying public the song had exposed them to. 'Coffee Shop' was more generic 1989-era funk rock made interesting by Kiedis' wired, paranoid-sounding vocal effects and Navarro's awkward guitar. Aside for an ill-fitting mid-song funk workout, the chorus also managed to rhyme 'coffee shop' and 'parking lot' with 'Iggy Pop'.

Written by Flea after he had been beaten up by rednecks who had taken umbrage at his pink Mohawk, 'Pea' saw a lo-fi acoustic turn by Flea (who had been making numerous home acoustic recordings over the previous couple of years, including a contribution to a tribute album of his beloved Germs), which sounded like it had been recorded first take. 'One Big Mob' bore the new influence of Navarro. Arty and layered like – unsurprisingly – Jane's, it was tempered in a way the Chili Peppers had never managed before, building up to a frantic peak. Again, it clocked in at over six minutes in length.

Next up was a track which included a dictaphone recording of Dave's little brother James. On 'One Big Mob', the guitarist was in a dilemma: with no Kiedis vocal to fill a particular moment, and no logical guitar solo to fill the slot, Navarro remembered a recording that he had made of James crying, with an idea that it might come in handy one day. "It seemed to fit the mood perfectly," he said.

Navarro later dismissed 'Walkabout' and it was easy to see why. Limp, inoffensively funky and name-checking didgeridoo's and aborigines, it was as pointless and crass as anything by Jamiroquai. 'Tearjerker' was read by some critics to be Kiedis' tribute to the recently-departed Kurt Cobain, an artist he admired a great deal but the lyrics were too oblique to identify the subject for certain. Musically, it was another sign that the Chili's were maturing, the sweeping strings reminiscent – unbelievably – of The Beatles.

For an album title track, 'One Hot Minute' was uncharacteristically dark and bore the echoes of grunge's bedraggled roar – it was a song not yet reached by sunlight. Nimbly avoiding more funk, Navarro piled on his guitars but they weren't enough – the song was symptomatic of a more general musical confusion which was veering from forced feelgood funk and darker moments like this. Both 'Falling Into Grace' and 'Shallow Be Thy Name' fell into funk mode again. 'Falling…' featured Navarro playing through a talkbox, an instrument pioneered in the rock world by the likes of Aerosmith's Joe Perry in the Seventies. It also featured chanting by the band's yoga instructor, Gurmukh Kaur Khalsa. The latter of the two songs showed the inspiration of Jane's Addiction more clearly – when Perry Farrell's mob played a sound bordering on funk metal, that is.

Thoughtfully composed yet containing liberal use of the word 'fuck', the album closer, 'Transcending' was the Red Hot Chilli Peppers' tribute to their friend River Phoenix. The song morphed into a howling tuneless ending that seemed to sum up the entire album. As the website allmusic.com put it: "Navarro's metallic guitar shredding should have added some weight to the Chili Peppers' punk-inflected heavy-guitar funk, but tends to make it plodding. By emphasizing the metal, the funk is gradually phased out of the blend, as is melody..."

Even the album's artwork was less colourful – less wilfully wacky – than previous releases. All lyrics were presented in neat calligraphy alongside children storybook pictures, the cover a lively illustration of an innocent girl making merry on a piano, a winged fairy by her side.

Only one song from 'One Hot Minute' made it onto the band's later 2003 *Greatest Hits* collection ('My Friends') and the album soon came to be regarded as the product of a band in flux, a band fighting for survival. Navarro had stepped into the breach, added new tones of colours to the band, and, despite his own battles with drugs, had given them reason to keep going. After all, in their previous two guitarists the band had already seen death and crippling addiction.

Being so diverse, the album confused many fans that were looking for a Slovak/Frusciante-style follow up to *Bloodsugarsexmagic*. Despite the pillorying that some critics gave it (perhaps unnecessarily harshly) it is often viewed with genuine affection by Peppers fans, who argued it was a creative moment in the band's history where they found the balance between superstardom and oblivion. There was no single-take recording mentality, and the lengthy layering of tracks and searching for appropriate lyrics undeniably resulted in a moody, melancholic piece.

The ghost of Kurt Cobain still haunted any band that were, like the Chili Peppers, trying to muscle their way through the corporate shit of the music business to create something genuinely stimulating and new. Cobain's struggle with addiction in many ways mirrored that of Kiedis, and at a time when fans, musicians and the industry as a whole were forced to re-assess themselves in the wake of Kurt's suicide, this was inevitably a critical point for the band.

Kiedis said in 2002 that the making of *One Hot Minute* was a troubled time for him personally. Clearly missing Frusciante in the band, and appearing to agree with the general consensus that this is one of their weakest albums, he remains today amazed when fans quote the album as a favourite. Flea, speaking during the tour to promote the album, prophetically focussed on the differences that Navarro brought to the group rather than particularly identifying them as benefits. He describes Navarro as "coming from his own trip... which was very different from the Chili Peppers."

As relationships with Kiedis in particular would sour, Navarro was well aware that theirs was a union that wouldn't last. Despite still being in possession of a vast and loyal following and a high profile, the Red Hot Chili Peppers were uneasily situated in the mid-Nineties music scene. *One Hot Minute* was emblematic of this period but it was a vital project in terms of seeing that the band could survive. Though an inferior work by their high standards, it can be seen as a stepping-stone to major achievements ahead. In Dave Navarro the Chilis had tried to find a rejuvenation that truly only came when Frusciante would finally re-join the band, but not before his own personal hell.

The fact that this proved to be Navarro's sole contribution to their recorded legacy could be seen as a shame by some observers. They had always had to move forward to survive, and many fans felt that Dave – had he stayed for a second album – would have taken them into a very different place musically. Others – especially after Woodstock II – felt that Dave was in fact the best live guitarist the band ever had: incendiary and passionate, inventive and alive. Sales of the new album, however, were not as impressive as the band, and their record label, had hoped for. The album debuted at #4 on the American, and #2 in the British charts, but sold nowhere near the quantity of the previous album. Recalling his exhaustion after their previous outing, and keen to spend more time with his growing daughter, Flea insisted that they tour less too. The outing to promote the album hit fewer cities than before, and by July 1996, as they entered the UK leg of the tour, it was already rumoured that Navarro was ready to go. Despite his bandmates' protestations to the contrary, Dave told the press that he often felt he didn't want to be in the band at all. "There's always some area of what we're doing... that I hate," he told *Kerrang!* with creditable honesty. "At times it's just the money that keeps me going."

Fortunately, there was more Chili Peppers' product to keep the flame alive. The album *Out In LA* was released in 1994, billed as a 'collection of rarities'. In fact, the majority of the record is comprised of average remixes, rough early demos of songs finished and polished elsewhere. Some commentators saw it as EMI ensuring that there was product in the marketplace when in actual fact the band almost didn't exist. One critic even suggested that the handwritten sleevenotes were better than the content of the album itself, but noted that the band's first demo (as 'Tony Flow And The Miraculously Majestic Masters of Mayhem') was an antique piece worthy of collection.

1994 also saw the release of *The Chase*, a Charlie Sheen action comedy movie featuring tattooed Renaissance Man Henry Rollins, and in which Flea and Kiedis had minor roles. Set up as weirdo truck drivers (the movie is little more than an entertaining collection of car chase opportunities), their highlight moment comes as they try to ram their truck into Sheen's vehicle.

The Chili Peppers have a history of acting in movies, as well as providing soundtrack music for them. Most of this is probably attributable to Kiedis' father Blackie Dammett, who – when Anthony was two years old – made a black and white movie called *The Hooligans*, that featured his young son (Blackie is also the *numero-uno* manager of the Chili Peppers' official web site). After his very early film roles in 1986, Anthony had appeared in Jeff Kanew's *Tough Guys*, the story of two elderly gangsters looking to stage one last heist. The movie was a delightful blend of Burt Lancaster and Kirk Douglas's collected years of experience in front of the camera. 1987's *Less Than Zero*, based upon the novel by *American Psycho* writer Brett Easton Ellis, wasn't a huge critical success, relying on too many loud party-and-attempts-to-shock scenes. Rich brats with too much time on their hands, sniffing too much coke and having too much sex, were never going to strike a chord with the general movie-going public. Appearing as 'musician #3,' Kiedis used the name Cole Dammett again in the credits, and Flea appeared briefly too, but the movie failed to create the controversy that the book on which it was based achieved - though in truth that was as much a marketing success as a quality work of literature. *Point Break* (1991) starring Patrick Swayze and Keanu Reeves as an FBI agent was an altogether better movie, an action flick from director Kathryn Bigelow (*Strange Days*, *Blue Steel*). Anthony spent two days on his role, and was quoted as saying he was "so happy when the two days were up and I went back to being in the band." Although he enjoys the acting experience, Anthony never loses sight of his day job.

Flea has appeared in a number of movies too. As mentioned is first role was in 1984's *Suburbia*, one of a bunch of highly fictionalised but nevertheless effective punks on the edge of society. That movie did become something of a 'must-see' for the late Eighties and Nineties. *Thrashin'*, from 1986, was a much more disposable affair, the plot-hungry tale of a bunch of character-less skateboard dudes led by Corey Webster (Joshua Brolin). If the movie has any value it is as a snapshot of skateboard life in the mid-Eighties, and retains something of a cult following as such.

One-time girlfriend Ione Skye played the joint lead in *Stranded*, a fun alien movie from 1987 in which Flea appeared as 'Jester the Alien' his puckish features squashed into what one reviewer called the 'most annoying' alien of the group. *Dudes* – from the director of *Suburbia* - was another punk movie, in which Flea – along with Jon Cryer and Daniel Roebuck – play three punks on a road trip from California to New York. 1988's *Let's Get Lost* was a well-received and moving bio-pic of legendary jazz trumpeter Chet Baker, who fell from a window to his death in 1988, in which Flea appeared as himself.

Still finding time to get before the movie cameras between Chili Pepper dates, Flea then slotted in as 'Floyd' in John Lafia's tongue-in-cheek *Blue Iguana*, a cult classic mixing Spaghetti Western with *film noir* and bags of style. Flea also appeared in the second and third films in the *Back To The Future* series, as well as *Motorama* and *My Own Private Idaho* alongside River Phoenix and Keanu Reeves (1991). Anthony had auditioned for *Idaho* along with Flea but – having been up for two days and – in his own words – being "psychologically shattered", he failed to get a part. In 1992, *Roadside Prophets* was released, and in 1993 Flea played an uncredited tattoo artist in Steve Rash's *Son In Law*. *Just Your Luck*, *Big Lebowski* and the fine Terry Gilliam version of Hunter S Thompson's *Fear And Loathing In Las Vegas* filled up the mid-Nineties for Flea the Actor, but in 1998 he landed a real gem of a part.

The Wild Thornberries was one of a whole spate of post-*Simpsons* family-based cartoon series that put quality writing, humour and all-age appeal back into children's television. The story of the Anglo-American family of wildlife film-makers who travel the world shooting footage of lions and cheetahs while engaging in adventures that Scooby Doo would die for, demanded a vocal talent to represent the wild-child adoptee of the family, 'Donny'. Flea landed the part, which transferred to the big screen in 2002, as well as a 2001 *The Origin of Donny* TV special.

As well as the *Thornberries* movies, other more recent roles in which Flea has appeared include parts in *Liar's Poker* with Richard Tyson (1999), *Goodbye, Casanova* (2000), *Psycho* (1999) and *Gen 13*, in which his voice-over featured as the comic book character 'Grunge.' It's true to say that Flea has never really set Hollywood alight as an actor, but his CV to date includes over twenty films, some of them very successful – a creditable tally given that the majority of rock stars-turned-actors make one or two half-decent films at most, and slide off the movie roller-coaster after directors realise that they may be hot property in the record stores but are not box-office material. Flea's billing has gradually been improved in each film he has made, and one day it seems entirely feasible that he may well find a lead part that achieves major creditable reviews and commercial success.

In May 1993, the Red Hot Chili Peppers were immortalised in the finest way when they appeared – stylised as all the characters in the show are, with yellow skin and wonderfully protruding upper lips – in an episode of the greatest television show of them all, *The Simpsons*. Many other celebrities have been involved in the show, from Paul and Linda McCartney, U2, the Rolling Stones to British Prime Minister Tony Blair. The Chili Peppers appeared in an episode where Krusty the Clown – Springfield's ubiquitous one-man entertainment industry – is bumped off the TV ratings by a staggeringly effective advertising campaign promoting Arthur Crandall and his ventriloquist dummy 'Gabbo.' Krusty's show is dumped, but Bart and Lisa Simpson enlist the help of Krusty's Hollywood pals to revive the programme. Hugh Hefner, Bette Midler and Elizabeth Taylor join the Chili Peppers in the campaign and – after a highly emotional TV special – Krusty is re-instated. Neatly, Crandall disappears for good as well.

The band was hugely delighted at their inclusion in the programme, and they looked good in yellow. Anthony's only complaint was that their tattoos were portrayed inaccurately.

CHAPTER 15

1995 saw the release of one of the biggest-selling albums in recent pop history, Alanis Morissette's *Jagged Little Pill*. Indeed, it remains the biggest selling album by a female artist –at 33 million copies – and also the biggest debut album of all-time. Inevitably, Morissette had her critics, some of whom said it was 'grunge-lite', a cleverly manufactured album to appeal to the prevailing alternative atmosphere yet also perfectly fit the mainstream radio's playlist criteria. Yet it wasn't just a record made by mainstream musicians – on one version of the stand-out track 'You Oughta Know' (later pressings also included a version with Morissette's studio band) Flea played bass and Dave Navarro played guitar. Despite his recent illness, Flea continued to be one of the hardest working bassists in rock. He was a guest on Cheikha Rimitti's album *Sidi Mansour*. Also, Rimitti, the 70-year old grandmother of Algerian dance music, featured Flea alongside the wonderful Robert Fripp, sometime King Crimson guru and one of rock's most influential, intellectual and idiosyncratic guitarists.

Over the years, Flea has guested on many albums and tracks by a plethora of different artists, including Johnny Cash's *Unchained*, Banyan's *Anytime At All*, and tracks by Mick Jagger, Action Figure Party, Government Mule, Jewel and Mike Watt. He is in demand as a session player for movie soundtracks too.

The irony is that one of the biggest criticisms of *One Hot Minute* was that it was a 'lazy' album, which saw it greeted with dismay in many quarters, labelled "puny", "arrogant" and "insecure" by critics, and demonstrating a this apparent laziness of attack after the long lay-off. For a band with such a charismatic and influential bass-player, for this department in particular to be singled out as weak must have hurt Flea.

In 1997, the band took time out from their endless touring schedule, playing just one show during the year, the Fuji Rock Festival in Japan. Hit by Typhoon Rosie, the gig was cut down to half its intended length when 80mph winds forced the band off stage. Roadies had to hold the on-stage gear down to stop them going into orbit, and the whole thing became too dangerous for even this band to risk. Dave told a journalist that from *Addicted To Noise* that he reckoned the gods of Mount Fuji "weren't interested in having western decadence turn a buck at the base of the holy spot!"

It was kind of symptomatic of where the band was at this time. They had already pulled out of the Tibetan Freedom Festival worried about being under-rehearsed (showing a conscience not usually found in rock stars). At this time, Anthony – something of a motor cycle connoisseur, owning a collection of classic and contemporary bikes – managed to negotiate his way off his Harley Davidson at some speed when he was in collision with a car in LA. He badly damaged his wrist (contradictory news reports suggested he broke eleven bones in it, while others referred just to a bad dislocation), though it could have been worse. Chad was out of action for a month on doctor's advice when he too managed to injure himself in a motorbike accident – the result for him was a damaged shoulder. More gigs – this time in Hawaii and Alaska were cancelled.

It wasn't just highway smashes that were diverting attention away from the band. Side projects pulled their attention all over the place too. Navarro and Flea played some sessions with Perry Farrell's latest incarnation, Porno for Pyros, cutting the track 'Hard Charger' that appeared on the soundtrack of the movie *Private Parts*. This led to live dates for the pair playing Porno and Jane's Addiction tracks. With three-quarters of Jane's Addiction together on the road, the time was right for a reform – or 'relapse' as it was entertainingly known in the music media. The Addiction's 'Relapse' was an appropriately named project, with Flea taking up the bass player's role. A 17-date tour and the *Kettle Whistle* album were the well-received result, and it seemed the Addiction were happy to settle comfortably into the shoes of their thirty-something audience. The album contained new tracks (including unreleased old material), live and studio out-takes, and demonstrated both that their break-up was creatively timely but that there was still gas in the tank for future work. *Three Days*, a 'rockumentary' account of the tour was made by Carter Smith and Kevin Ford. The 90-minute film explores the Rabelaisian, Fellini-like excesses of a band on tour, and sneaks private peeks at the work of the individuals involved, including Flea and Dave.

In 1998, EMI released *Under The Covers*, a collection of the Chili's cover versions, and a valuable sidelong glance both at the band and at their influences. Tracks by Hendrix and Dylan sat alongside The Stooges and Elton John. Punk, funk, pop and rock – the album clearly showed a well-rounded Chili Peppers. The concept of a covers album was far from new – David Bowie's *Pin-Ups* from 1973 being a classic of the genre, John

Lennon's *Rock 'n' Roll* (from the same year) another. The format allows an artist to do a number of things: he can pay genuine homage to work that has inspired him; he can earn royalties for the authors of the songs he represents; and a band can loosen up on someone else's material.

Early in 1998 Anthony was saddened to hear of the death of another influence on his life. Sonny Bono, one half of Sixties pop duo Sonny and Cher, died in a skiing accident in Tahoe, where as a child Kiedis himself had holidayed with the singer. Bono, long-separated from Cher, had gone into politics after his music career quietened down. He had been a close friend of Anthony's father and they had even used Sonny's Bel Air address when trying to find a school for Anthony after his move to live with his father. The whole world was saddened by the loss of Sonny, whose TV show with Cher had been the top-rated on American television at the time, and who had made some of the best flower-pop of the Sixties.

In March, Dave Navarro unveiled a side project, Spread, an instrumental band including Chad on drums and Dave on guitar, with their first release to be called *Unicorns & Rainbows: The Pelican.* By 2001 the project had become *Trust No One.* He talked about being burned out, the rock and roll process and lifestyle having taken their toll on him. More tellingly, he spoke about the Peppers' next album, by then already reasonably advanced, and when asked how it might be different from *One Hot Minute* he said: "This material might actually be good." Clearly, the band was in poor shape. Navarro went on to tell *Guitar* magazine that he couldn't predict a bright future for the band: "With our luck that would be like shooting myself in the foot," he moaned. Navarro's time in the band typified their blackest period in terms of image. His own punk/metal/gothic leanings were reflected in the band's leather, black nails and make-up, which was pretty much a rite of passage for the group.

Less than a month later, an announcement from the band alerted the public to Navarro's departure, citing his commitment to the Spread project as the reason for his leaving. Anthony was keen to stress that Dave's time in the band had been fun, and that the Chili Peppers still loved him. Flea later summed up that phase by saying to VH-1 how "we came from completely different musical backgrounds, Dave's a great guy, he makes a great rock star and a helluva rock guitar player, but for some reason we could never all get on the same page." Dave agreed that the parting was mutual and affectionate: "When I was seventeen, the time had come for me to leave the comfort and safety of the (family) nest... I knew that in my absence the love my father had for me would be no different than my love for him. The only difference that I can see in this case is that my father would never have suggested the light bulb costumes..." In one interview Dave talked of both his work in the Chili Peppers and that of Jane's Addiction with an interesting comparison: "(Jane's Addiction) created its art through a self-destructive process, whereas The Chili Peppers create (theirs) through the healing process." Yet again, it was clear that The Red Hot Chili Peppers as a band was about the interaction and the positive forces between four individuals, rather than the differences. It's hard, however, for some critics not to sometimes perceive their apparent revolving-door personnel as something quite the opposite.

Rock and roll bands are often rats' nests of infighting and back-biting, and genuinely harmonious splits are comparatively rare. There were unsubstantiated press rumours that Dave had been effectively dumped by Anthony Kiedis, and that Flea was voted the bearer of the bad news. Music mag *Kerrang!* quoted a passage from Navarro's yet-to-be-published memoirs in which Navarro claimed to have been excluded from a management meeting during which his future with the band was discussed. Kiedis was reported by some to have an issue with "chemistry that isn't working", a two-year-long problem that effectively meant he neither agreed with Navarro's contribution to the band nor particularly wanted it to continue. 'Under these circumstances," wrote Navarro, "I felt upset and humiliated." Having spoken with Flea, and finally confronting Kiedis himself, Navarro found the singer and writer was not forthcoming about the real reasons for wanting him out, allegedly falling back on stock responses and things he "could not put into words."

So, yet another "exploding guitarist" moment for the band. Rick Rubin added his own take on the situation, later telling *Spin* magazine that Anthony and Navarro were poles apart, personality-wise: "Dave is dark-humoured, dark-souled," he said. "Anthony doesn't appreciate that." Navarro remained remarkably un-bitter about the whole series of events, later telling journalists that – in addition to his continuing respect for all the members of the band – his favourite member was John Frusciante.

In the fall of 1998 rumours began to spread in the British tabloid press that Kiedis was dating ex-Spice Girl singer Melanie Chisholme. While one newspaper reported the couple as an established item, another – on the same day – paired her off with another "secret lover." What was clear was that Anthony and 'Sporty' Mel C did in fact meet backstage after a Spice Girls gig in Los Angeles, and it appears that they did meet more than once. Despite admitting such bare facts in interviews, Melanie never confirmed that the couple were anything more than friends, and the story-that-never-quite-was passed into tabloid history.

At one of these gigs, Melanie also met Flea's daughter Clara, who made it to her dad's gigs when school allowed. Having joined her school choir for the actual vocals on the track, she had also appeared in a video clip for 'Aeroplane' from *One Hot Minute*; rather brilliantly, she also designed some merchandise images for the band when very young, and was an all-out member of the touring party whenever she wanted to be.

The single for 'Aeroplane' was a good example of how the Chilis were still concerned about keeping things real despite their escalating fame and fortune. Despite the band being unsure of the success of the video for 'Aeroplane', it was one of their most entertaining promo clips to date. The whole piece is wrapped up in a large chunk of kitsch and Thirties movie glamour (the clip is based upon the kind of major set-piece action that typified Busby Berkely movies). The footage combines glamorous but gum-chewing Mexican women, synchronised swimmers, a set based upon a stylised airport design and Flea's daughter Clara with her school friends dressed-up as little aeroplanes (she's the one in the middle)! In the 2003 release of the band's *Greatest Hits* video collection, they talked of the huge expense that the video entailed. Nothing on the shot was hired – everything was purpose built – except for the swimming pool itself. On one of Hollywood's oldest sound stages, the pool alone cost $20,000 to hire. Such was the cost that the band and director (Gavin Bowden again) decided to forego heating the water, which would have added even more expense – so all the dives and swimming sequences were made into icy cold water!

CHAPTER 16

There was a headrush of excitement in the media and the Chili fanbase alike when Karen Moss, Senior Vice-President of Warner Bros Records announced that Dave Navarro was to leave the Peppers – to be replaced by none other than John Frusciante. For fans and observers from afar, this was big news, a new twist in the soap opera of this most troubled of bands. Reflecting on how John's return could fill a void that had been opened up by his untimely departure that morning in Japan, Anthony said: "when you have that ultimate intimate experience as we had with John, (afterwards) we just didn't now what to do, it just didn't feel right, something was amiss." Not anymore. John was back and it was one helluva cause for celebration. Frusciante had been an absentee Chili for six years.

However, behind this apparent celebration, there was a personal hell. Frusciante's time away from the Red Hot Chili Peppers had seen a dreadful slide into substance abuse, heroin addiction and virtual death. He had produced two solo albums, but little else. Warner A&R Vice President David Katznelson pointed how great a move Frusciante's re-joining the band was: "To get him back… is a good thing for them," he said to journalists. "He wrote the music for 'Under The Bridge' and 'Breaking The Girl'. It's great to get him in a room and hear him play the original version… it's beautiful!"

That the band existed for him to rejoin at all was down to Kiedis, Flea and Smith's maintaining faith in its concept, working through what was deemed a "year of nothingness" before Frusciante came home. Kiedis had taken a reflective time-out in India – unhelpful rumours abounded that this was in order to quit heroin again, though this was both denied and untrue. Swimming about in the Ganges, Kiedis found some spiritual rest there, impressed by the notion that that famous waterway is in part a river and in part, so legend has it, a mother who will love and protect its children. Thrown around and into huge boulders by the currents of the river, he remained unharmed and returned from the trip chilled and ready to rock again. Flea, meanwhile, had been doing some travelling of his own, heading out to Costa Rica, with a biography of Che Guevara to read.

Painting and writing had occupied John almost more than playing guitar during the years out of the band. The voices in his head that he refers to as "spirits", and that he has heard since he was a child, were getting worse. At one point he said that there were *400* of them in his mind at the same time. John knew that some of his ghosts were there to help him and some were there to harm him – one of his biggest problems throughout the period was knowing which ones were which. Frusciante's ghosts and spirits felt so much more real than his 'real' life that they became his best friends. "I was so happy someone was visiting," he said of this deeply troubled period of his young life, "I'd make food for them." When they left him, he said, he would cry.

Never more than one bad fix away from a fatal overdose, Frusciante had told one reporter that he didn't care if he lived or died. At one point his house burned down, but after it was rebuilt, it was rumoured that Frusciante stopped making payments and it was taken away from him again. Conforming to the model of star-junky-corpse, John moved into the legendary Chateau Marmont hotel, home to rock stars and movie stars and only a few years back the scene of John Belushi's fatal demise. Gram Parsons, Jim Morrison and Led Zep had all rented there. Rake-thin and dressed in rags, he was a pathetic figure (amazingly, despite his problems with this drug, Anthony's physique has always managed to remain relatively superb, a testament to his hard work in the gym and increasingly healthy outlook on life). After a great deal of work on his behalf, Frusciante's lawyer raised the money to get his house back for him, but it was unfortunately sold on the day the money was raised. "That was fine with me," John told the alarmed press, "because that was 50,000 extra bucks I could spend on heroin."

Like drummer Jack Irons years before, Frusciante withdrew so far from what was once his favourite band on the planet that he claimed not to have even heard *One Hot Minute*. "It got into my head," he told journalist David Fricke "that stardom was something evil." Where his band-mates were unashamedly happy to admit that the commercial rewards of success were worth the effort, Frusciante had felt as though he had sold out to commercialism: "I had to be extra-humble, extra-anti-rock star," he said.

John was a classic junky. At the depths of his addiction, he still wondered how on earth he could ever have lived a life *without* drugs. No matter how far he fell, he constantly came back to the realisation that life on Planet Narcotic was better than life on Planet Earth. Indeed, unlike many users who slip into heroin by default, Frusciante has spoken often of a deliberate moment when he chose to become an addict. "It was a clear decision," he said. "I was very sad, and I was always happy when I was on drugs... (I thought I) should be on drugs all the time. I was always really proud to be an addict." His ghosts told him that he should take heroin constantly for six years. He wilfully became totally dependent on the substance that was killing him.

Suffering from depression to exacerbate his addiction, the guitarist had lost many friends – either to the junky graveyard in the sky or because they couldn't be around him any longer. He had witnessed River Phoenix's fatal demise on that fateful night at The Viper Room, and Phoenix had been a big supporter of his solo work. Yet even Phoenix's death failed to set alarm bells off in John's head. He and Flea had remained close friends, and although the band was hopelessly busy after 'Under The Bridge' started to hit and the Lollapalooza tour beckoned, Flea would come round to John's place in the Hollywood Hills and the friends would play guitars together. It is possible that the guitarist's return to the band was as a result of Flea talking to him during this literally dangerous period. It was certainly Flea who first voiced the idea of bringing him back on board, but he and Kiedis reckoned the chances of the thing working out were "a million to one." Even Flea became reluctant to call round to visit John. Having lost Hillel to the drug, it was painful to watch John on the same slide downhill. Drugs for Flea weren't an issue – he never needed them. As with Slovak, John seemed to need heroin like he needed air to breathe.

John's guitar playing had been much neglected during his years in the wilderness, but the faith of his former bandmates was enough to get him through: "it felt so good to have friends who really believed in me when nobody else did," he told *Kerrang!* when talking about his rebirth in the Chili Peppers.

He had done some work, however, while the heroin chewed at his body and mind. John's first solo album was conceived and recorded while he was still a member of the Chili Peppers, and he continued working on it after leaving the band. While its creator balanced somewhere between narcotic auto-pilot and self-destruct, *Niandra LaDes And Usually Just A T-Shirt* was released on American records in 1994, produced by Rick Rubin. It was recorded on four-track porta-studios. Encouraged by friends River Phoenix (who appears on the album, his voice reversed and interspersed with John's on the track 'Bought Her Soul'), Perry Farrell and Butthole Surfer Gibby Haynes, the album is really the sum of two parts. *Niandra LaDes...*, largely recorded during time off from the Chili Peppers, is a 12-song cycle of navel-gazing self-examination, while *Usually Just A*

T-Shirt is a 13-track series of more experimental music, John playing loose guitar and piano throughout. Frusciante's voice struggled, though it combined with the unusually frank music tracks to create something moving and undeniably haunting, albeit patchy. It's probably true to say that many people bought the album because of who had made it, only to put it to one side after one or two listens. It's probably also true that, ten years after its release, more and more people have pulled it off the shelf and given it a second listen. Like so many 'outsider' albums made by established stars – Lou Reed's *Metal Machine Music* being a classic example – time and re-assessment make it a much better record. Original and refreshing, dreadful and unlistenable at the same time, the album is filled with astonishing ideas, regardless of the frame of mind of John when he originally conceived them. John's playing is not great throughout the album, but there are moments of great harmonic simplicity that are deeply touching and affecting.

He dedicated the album to Clara Balzary, Flea's little girl. "She's the strongest person I've ever met," said John, who – surviving one of the most extreme intakes of heroin – was pretty much an expert on inner strength. More than anything, John's solo projects kept him working, and working maybe kept him alive. He learned more about sound textures and the 'feel' of his music, escaping the slavish technique that many of his peers employed. John held the album dear, even after his return to the Chili Peppers. Indeed, tracks such as 'Your Pussy Glued' and 'Building on Fire' became part of the live set on the later *Californication* tour, and were greeted warmly by the fans that had taken the trouble to understand this part of the man's work. All credit too to the rest of the Chili Peppers for embracing his solo work in this way.

Niandra LaDes... was not a raging success, selling in the tens of thousands rather than the millions, but it was a motivational exercise for Frusciante, helping focus his creativity throughout what anyone else would have seen as the worst period of his life. The project clearly gave Frusciante both the opportunity to 'be smaller,' and to escape pop and enter a world of more experimental music - to be himself. Unfortunately, it also gave him an income to spend on his narcotic intake, and with only royalty cheques to support his spending of anything up to $500 a day, every dime helped. A film made by Gibby Haynes and sent to journalists in the promotional push for *Niandra LaDes...* showed a wounded, unhappy man surrounded by disturbing graffiti and rambling to the camera. When press came to the house to interview him about his solo album, he managed to present a semblance of normality, but things were far from normal.

Frusciante OD'd in February 1996. Clinically dead, John's body apparently contained a little over 10% of the blood it should have done, but according to *Kerrang!* his response to being revived and given a blood transfusion was to get straight back out to fill up on drugs. Again, not unheard of in rock star and addict circles. For Anthony, who knew the difficulties that John was facing, it was a terrifying time. "I thought I had lost a friend forever and I didn't want him to die, so I prayed, 'Please don't let John die.'" Flea too was terrified and as he was around John a lot, he could see each day take its toll on the increasingly weak friend. "I stayed in touch with him through the whole thing and it was difficult to be around him. I just thought he was going to die, I was *sure* John was going to die." Perhaps most frighteningly of all, John was contemplating suicide: "I had just deteriorated so much that I just wanted to die, I just wanted a gun bad so I could shoot myself, I'd really lost the will to live completely, my heart had broken completely."

Reporter Robert Wilonsky famously visited John at this time and found a pitiful wreck of a man, spattered with blood, his teeth rotted away and fingernails all but gone. His lips were coated with dried saliva, his feet and ankles burned by cigarette ash that he hadn't noticed, his body covered in bruising. To this day, the scars of needles ravage John's arms, where fumbling fingers have clumsily plunged injected narcotics into exhausted viens. By this stage, he didn't try to hide his problem away – when asked by that Dutch documentary team who filmed this quite disturbing interview with an incoherent and clearly very unwell Frusciante, John told them why he was taking heroin: "A way of making you stay in touch with beauty instead of letting the ugliness of the world corrupt your soul."

Unbelievably, from here he got worse. Trying to kick the heroin by turning to crack and cocaine, he simply immersed himself further in all three. Valium and alcohol fuelled the descent. Perhaps most remarkably of all, it was only when one of John's ghosts told him that now was not the time to die that he resolved to do something. Promising himself a final, fatal return to heroin if it didn't work out, John checked into a clinic, suddenly determined to clean up.

John had started wearing unkempt little beards to cover the bruising from the dental work that reputedly cost him $70,000 to fix his mouth. This was said to have included the process of having bone transplanted from his hip to the jaw so that there was something to fix his new set of teeth into. John also went through periods when he owed large amounts of money to dealers, and often had to borrow. At one point he owed $30,000 and, reportedly, there was a death threat against him.

Frusciante's second solo album *Smiles From The Streets You Hold* was released in 1997, still a long and troubled two years before rejoining the Chili Peppers. At this point John was surviving on supplement tablets designed for invalids, barely eating regular food at all. Put out on the Birdman label the album was a mixture of old, unreleased 1995 material, outtakes and even earlier stuff. The title song was a very intense moment," John told James Rotundi from *Guitar Player* magazine, "because I was having verbal communication with the spirits while I was recording."

Released purely to fund his addiction, the album was later deleted at his own request. A difficult album – screamed lyrics, extended noise and often incomprehensible guitar – it nevertheless contained a few worthy moments recorded on four-track recorders with low quality sound reproduction. The album could certainly not be listened to within the Chili Peppers' canon – this was something perhaps for followers of Captain Beefheart, Syd Barrett, and Zappa rather than *Bloodsugarsexmagic*, but to be honest, not easy for them either. John not only did all the music but also painted the pictures that decorate the album sleeve. Painting was a worthy therapy for John at this time, and he even considered giving up the guitar to become a painter full time, having an exhibition at the Zero One gallery on Melrose Avenue. Thankfully John changed his mind, but he did spend time looking at the works of the great artists of the past and present, including Leonardo da Vinci, dadaist Marcel Duchamp and Vincent van Gogh.

John finally concluded that he really just didn't have the technical know-how to cut it as a painter. He told one journalist that he finally realised that his guitar was his paintbrush, and that he could paint colours: "I try to be sure that every single note has the same importance as every colour in a painting (would)," he said. "I am very proud of being able to express myself with my guitar, and to be able to say almost everything I want with it."

Zipping forward in the band's chronology for a moment, John's third solo album, *To Record Only Water For Ten Days*, was released in 2001, two years after the Chili Peppers' *Californication*. Finally John would produce a piece of work that was a worthy testament to his remarkable recovery and to his equally remarkable talent. John put the album together during and after the *Californication* sessions. Frusciante showed influences as varied as Joy Division, Tricky, Depeche Mode and New Order. It was a nod to Eighties synth pop, but also showed the influence of the songwriters who had first inspired John – Lou Reed, David Bowie and Syd Barrett, late of Pink Floyd.

John was simply glad – and lucky – to be still alive and writing, glad to be contributing. The album's title came from a revelation in which the guitarist heard a voice tell him that, if he recorded only the sounds of water, the playback sounds would – as fresh water does – fill the air with positivity, freshness and hope. For a man who had skirted so closely around death and despair, the symbolism was clearly redolent. While the generally unpolished production harks back to the experimental sounds of John's earlier solo outings, this is clearly a superior collection of material, his songwriting truly to the fore, with luscious string sections and passionate vocals.

"I have two musical lives," Frusciante told *The Toronto Sun*. "If Anthony or Flea made solo records it wouldn't sound anything like the Chili Peppers." Frusciante had been writing songs since he was eleven years old: for him his solo albums represent the songwriter in him, whereas his work in the Chili Peppers represented his work as a guitar-player. The album drew heavily on John's years of addiction for its vision and tone. During this period Frusciante had achieved little in a material sense, but he did find more and more of an inner life.

Most of the album was written on acoustic guitar between November 1999 and April 2000. John had begun carrying an acoustic with him during the *Californication* tour, and the habit of carrying one around both entertained him but also gave him a revised format in which to experiment. One of his formative influences, Pink Floyd's Syd Barrett, had been an acoustic inspiration for him when he began to play the guitar again after the long lay-off. The working title of *Breaking The Girl* had indeed been *12-String*, and John was clearly happy to be re-united properly with the instrument on which he first learned to play.

John spoke of the album with great affection. "The fact that I'm now able to write an album that can make people happy when they hear it is a great accomplishment for me," he told *Guitar World*. He was happy to explain some of the recording tricks employed in the album's construction. The slide guitar/voice sound in 'Going Inside', for example, was created by inserting moments of silence into the vocal track, while the opening moments of the song feature the voice sent through a compressor and overdriven to the point where even the *Guitar World* journalist had thought it was a guitar sound.

Clean of narcotics (he went into rehab in 1997), John had a route through music to bring all his demons into the world and to make sense of them. Although off the heroin, he could still talk rationally about a fourth dimension world in which sounds, shapes and colours make the landscape and where music and art are the clouds and the grass, and of his ability to interact with this world and to bring its flavours into his own. John is a remarkable individual, a real survivor, and a crucial part of a story that is about exactly that: survival.

John himself has often denied that his contribution to the Peppers is the key to their success, but does acknowledge that with him in the band the mix that they come up with is more creative collectively. "I play a certain way in this band that I can't repeat outside of it," he told one journalist, and it was clear from the Chili Peppers' first album with him back in the fold – described by most observers as a 'comeback' album – that his contribution was immediate and had a shatteringly effect. He later said that he never listened to *One Hot Minute*, and that nobody had ever come up with a convincing reason why he should, and many people observed that the process of John coming back into the band seemed seamless, as though he had never been away.

CHAPTER 17

It's certainly true that the future would have been very different if John had not come back into the Red Hot Chili Peppers. We've already seen that the band managed only one concert in 1997. Dave Navarro's departure in April 1998, despite all the musical differences, left the band in tatters. Flea apparently announced that if they didn't try and get Frusciante back in the band he would leave too. The band was unsure of what the hell this might mean, but they knew that if they didn't do something they were finished. John was the *only* guy who could fill the guitar role in the band after Slovak, and they knew it. As Flea contacted John and they started to talk about rejoining the band, Anthony visited him and began to heal the wounds of their not having spoken for years. Anthony was highly doubtful of the chances of this whole thing coming off, but if Flea thought it would work Anthony would go along with it. And he certainly hadn't stopped loving John – the issue was only one of whether the band could work again with him in it.

Kiedis and Flea were right to be unsure of the effect Frusciante would have if he came back, and wrong in their assessment that there perhaps could be friction. He owed thousands of dollars to dealers, his arms were covered in the hideous marks left behind by years of shooting up. But the reaction they got the day they actually asked him to rejoin his favourite band ever should have given them all the reassurances they needed: "I went to his house and asked him what he thought about being in the band again and his face went bright red and he said, 'Oh, I think that would be a good idea!'" said Flea.

Even if his re-joining the band was his way of working his way out of these depths, the fortunate fact is that from day one it worked out like a dream and John's welcome return set the band alight once more. "Right now," said Kiedis, "it's working like crazy..." – recognizing that it was best not to look too far into the future. Flea was shocked by the dramatic turnaround in his friend's life: "Now he is one of the most focussed dedicated, awesome awe-inspiring artists that I know, someone that I am absolutely challenged to play with because he is *so* good, *so* smart and *so* on it amazing, really *amazing*." In a reference to his genuine fear that Frusciante would slip away just like Hillel had, Anthony said, "it was really the best, it was like having someone die in your family and then come back to life."

Kiedis continued on VH-1 by saying, "(John is) a genius, he has that mad scientist, guitar, art, love, spirit, genius in him, but he doesn't know how to drive a car, he doesn't have a credit card, he doesn't function on the same road as the rest of the world which is what makes him great."

Ironically, at this point Frusciante seemed to have a new inner strength and Anthony talked of how it was his own fragility that he feared for more than that of his friend. Anthony was also clean and appeared in the media to have a genuine sense of perspective and control over his life – articulate as ever, he was perhaps at his most fascinating when talking about his difficult experiences: "(I had to) get honest with myself," he told VH-1, "you are just a liar if you think you can go out and do that and not destroy your life and everything around you, whereas before (being clean) I kept thinking somehow I can get away with it, I can control it, which is basically lying to myself."

John had found a route to escape his drugs hell – ironically the very thing that may have disillusioned him so much in the first instance: the band, his music. Although he claimed to still love the feelings and experiences he had while on drugs, he knew that today he had to try and recreate those feelings through his music and not through narcotics. "At nineteen," he said, "I might have looked like a stud, but I was a weakling inside. I wasn't proud of who I was then. And now I am proud of who I am."

In June, John appeared with the rest of the band on an LA radio show, his first outing with the group since 1992. A week later they played a comeback gig at the 9:30 Club in Washington, and followed that by appearing at the Tibetan Freedom Concert the next day. Summer was spent jamming in Flea's garage, with a diversion to the Reading Festival in the UK in August, to which Flea's mom brought his daughter Clara. Jams quickly produced thirty or forty songs, with the established formula of having the grooves all worked out before the band entered the studio. The Red Hot Chili Peppers were back.

Kiedis was ecstatic at the slice of energy that Frusciante injected back into the group: "When John gets excited, he's like a billion volts of electricity," he told *Rolling Stone*. "...when he hit that first chord it was so perfect – this blend of sounds from these people who I hadn't hear play together for so long." Flea was working through emotional problems of his own, having broken up with his girlfriend of five years. Ultimately the studio and the making of *Californication* was his saviour. This time he found the discipline of the recording studio helped him put the emotional horrors behind him, and he was given great support by his own daughter, who showed a maturity way beyond her years in talking him down from his bouts of perceived failure.

The title of the next Red Hot Chili Peppers' album, one that some observers might never be made, was *Californication*. The title song has a double reference. One clear message is a glance back over the shoulders of the band to their hard-partying days of yore, when fornication was a pre-requisite for Californian living. More tellingly, the second dates back to a trip that Anthony made to Indonesia after John left the band. In village markets where even Coca Cola had failed to penetrate the local consciousness, Kiedis found Red Hot Chili Pepper and Guns N' Roses T-shirts, Hollywood movies and western music CDs. It seemed to Anthony that California's achievements in marketing its wares worldwide mirrored the entire process by which the West as a whole now colonised other parts of the world. As Britain, hung off the very edge of Europe, had once ruled the waves through its navy, its civil service and its Anglican Church, now California – perched similarly out on the furthest western limb of the USA, ruled the roost. The cover shot cleverly represents a Californian dream home, and subtly inverts the details so that the swimming pool contains the sky and vice versa. Whatever the listener's pre-conceived idea of California, this is clearly a subversion of the norm.

Rick Rubin was back in his familiar seat at the production desk, and he noticed a stark difference in the band. In particular, Rubin pointed out that Frusciante's creative imagination was as important a part of the band as his guitar playing. Rick brought the band together in Studio Two at Ocean Way Recording studios in Los Angeles. They were in the same room in which The Beach Boys' classic album *Pet Sounds* was devised, and Frank Sinatra had recorded in here too. Amazingly, in five days the basic tracks were under way and in less than a month the band had cut nearly thirty songs for the new album.

Flea, Frusciante and Smith laid down the instrumental tracks at a furious pace, and Kiedis would add lyrics to them as the sessions progressed. Rick Rubin ran the sessions at a breakneck speed too, with Anthony hard-pressed to keep up with the creative surge that Frusciante brought back to the outfit. The majority of tracks grew from intensive jamming, and Rubin thought he saw the same intense energy, the same commitment, that he'd witnessed for *Bloodsugar...*: "It's the closest they've come to that same energy," he told reporters. Despite Flea's domestic turmoil – the album was finished in record time. "When... we're only concerned with trying to get good performances it's very easy,' Chad Smith told *Kerrang!* "The worst thing about drugs is that people get consumed by them and nothing else matters. Things get done, but it takes a really long time."

Sometimes clean-up time can spoil a band's creative energy. Where cocaine sucks the life-blood out of its users, heroin – however physically and emotionally destructive – often heightens the creative process. Keith Richards famously noted that while at the depth of his heroin abuse he not only made *Exile On Main Street* – for many the greatest Stones album of all – but he also learned to ski! Often when artists clean up their music suffers: compare *Exile...* with the 1980 Stones offering *Emotional Rescue*. Also, in the 70s, David Bowie descended into a nightmare world of cocaine addiction and paranoia while producing his most challenging and durable music. When he reappeared, a reformed figure, in 1983, it was with the anodyne, commercially gigantic *Let's Dance,* an artistic nadir.

But for the Chili Peppers, free of serious narcotics use, *Californication* was the peak of their career to date, artistically and commercially – *Bloodsugarsexmagik* included. Kiedis appeared to have a sense of a fateful presence looking over the band. He told journalists that he felt there was "something in the air" that allowed the album to happen. In truth, the major development was that rather than working through improvised jams that demonstrated their musicianship but not always their writing abilities, on *Californication* they hit the golden button more often than on any previous album. Throughout the album there are rock-hard, catchy choruses, gentle ballads, Nirvana-like shifts from loud to soft and back again, edgy, funked-up numbers that looked over their shoulders at albums past but around the next corner too.

In keeping with the technological advances made since their last major studio release, *Californication* was released early on the web, a way to "get the new music directly to their fans," as their management company put it. Three new songs a day were previewed online between June 4th and June 11th, with the album itself available twice over the same period. Debuting at #3 in the chart in June 1999, it was clear that although the release of a new Peppers' album might not have been quite the event it had been a few years earlier, there was still a broad fan base there for them. Kiedis, with freshly bleached, short-cut hair (ritually removed in September 1998), presented a new profile that spoke volumes of his renewed attitudes and cleaner life-style. "I was definitely going through a change," he told a reporter later. "It was a whole new era for myself and the band." Yet the songs on the album are lonelier than before, more reflective. Visitors to the band's website could watch the progress of Anthony being shorn of his legendary long locks in a series of photos that followed the job being done. Bare-chested, occasionally blonde, muscular and leaping around the stage with abandon, Kiedis has on more than one occasion born a remarkable similarity to the granddaddy of punk, Iggy Pop – to the extent that one interviewer actually asked him if The Ig was his father! Needless to say, the two are not related.

'Scar Tissue' was the first single release, and its video summed up neatly the point on their journey that the band had reached while also cleverly presenting their much more current visual image – at times Anthony's long hair seemed to put him back in time to the late Eighties nadir of funk-metal such as Extreme. Directed by photographer Stephen Sednaoui – who had previously directed Madonna and Kylie Minogue videos – the clip opens with John Frusciante driving the band across the desert in an old open-top sedan. John is one of the world's least enthusiastic drivers, and talking about the clip in 2003 he explained how this was really only about the second time he had ever driven. The imagery of the video is simple but effective – the band are on the road, badly bruised and covered in bandages and blood-stains; but most of all they are together in the car and are still alive. It's not hard to interpret this as representing John's return and the band's ability to survive together against the odds. Throughout the video they play damaged instruments – Flea's bass has no strings, John's guitar is broken at the neck, and at the end of the clip John throws his broken guitar away, symbolic perhaps of his disowning that broken past, ready to embrace the future that the vehicle in which they travel leads them to. Anthony gave a hint to the meaning of the title, when he referred to it as a metaphor for "just having lived your life."

And what an album. From the ominous sounding guitars, cocksure bass and beats and lilting chorus, 'Around The World' re-announced the band's return in style. The Red Hot Chili Peppers had hardly alienated their fan base, but in an industry driven by sales figures, by the end of the Nineties their stock was plummeting. A band famed for a clutch of great singles, live shows and one truly great album were possibly no longer a bankable band. Until now…

Apparently, the video for 'Around The World' accompanying its release as a single was not their favourite. The band's fourth video with Stephane Sednaoui, a blue-haired Flea and Co. are represented in a series of stunning morph-like images, where their bodies superimposed on to one-another's, or onto multiple images of themselves. Alongside this, Anthony makes love to an ethereal, electronically-created woman-figure, and both Stephane and the band felt that this intruded upon the morphing images that should have been developed more themselves, as they create a stunning visual effect and a suitable metaphor for the shifting personalities of the four members of the band.

Back again to the album, after the surging infectious floor-filler of 'Around The World' – complete with a gratifyingly over-amplified bass sound mid-song and Kiedis deliberately nonsensical lyrics - 'Parallel Universe' was equally as refined. Over a sturdy Chad Smith backbeat, the band crafted a song that was coincidentally perfect for American rock radio – downbeat verse, uplifting hummable chorus, thrilling FX-laden finale. Clearly in their lengthy absence, Red Hot Chili Peppers had been taking stock of their situation and had returned with a new found sense of melody and the ability to abandon musical indulgence in favour of some stone-cold classic songs.

The lead single 'Scar Tissue' was mellow, quietly remorseful and an insight into the soul of the band. Frusciante's stirring wistful guitars and harmonising made for a song that undoubtedly rates as one of the band's finest moments. All sorts of meanings could be invested in the song's introspective lyrics – lyrics which were arguably the band's most poignantly poetic to date - the 'Scar Tissue' in question might well have been a reference to the guitarist scar-addled arms; war wounds from his crack/heroin addiction. Either way, as Kiedis and Frusciante harmonised over a gentle backdrop as warm-sounding as mid-afternoon rays of Californian sunshine, it was clear the band had turned a corner, moved on to the next level. 'Scar Tissue' was the song that showed the world that the sock-wearing, funk-obsessed jokers were long gone. With Frusciante having survived a brush with death and the series of below par-performances and releases in the mid-Nineties, the Red Hot Chili Peppers had matured into a fine cohesive unit once again. With *Californication* they had achieved consistency, creating a complete work with a definite sound and discernible themes.

A baleful ballad, 'Otherside' perfectly encapsulated this new-found – no other word for it – maturity and thoughtfulness. The Chili's were looking inside themselves and reporting back on what they saw through a series of such semi-ballads with strong, accessible choruses like this one – clearly a winning formula as 'Otherside' went on to become another huge international hit single. 'Get On Top' ' was the type of sexually-charged, lascivious funk that was to be found on every Chili's album to date, its title unabashedly alluding to nothing other than bedroom gymnastics, a sound to appease the Chili Peppers old guard. Yet the video for its release as a single was most innovative and clearly offered no solace for the pining funk-metal frat fans of old. Jonathan Dayton and Valerie Faris came to direct a whole series of clips for the band, and on 'Otherside' they produced a mesmeric video. The images are based upon ideas from German Expressionist cinema, Henky Penky's *Bloodsugarsexmagic* tongue images, the works of artists Man Ray and MC Escher and a movie that Flea remembered seeing late one night while the band were on tour. The film shows the band playing a number of non-instruments. Instead of his guitar, John plays a long rope with only one string; Chad drums like a surrealist vibe-player in the centre of three revolving circles; Flea plucks telegraph wires instead of bass strings as he sways in the air. This was a crazy and creative video, typical of the inventive work of its directors. It also marked another step up in *maturity* for the Chilis. Yet, this album had still more up its sleeve.

'Californication' was another album – indeed, *career* - highlight – and an infinitely far greater title track than that of 'One Hot Minute'. Lyrically it was strong too, Kiedis offering a poetic insight into a darker state of mind… and a state. In combining their vocal love and appreciation of sex and the sunshine of California, the pun of the title summed up the Chili Peppers perfectly and was too good to pass up on as an album title.

'Easily' was another classy album track. Where once the Chili's book-ended their stand-out songs with one-minute sub-punk bursts or tuneless funk now they were filling the gaps with songs that worked in their own right: songs to proud of. And, once again, far from being cringe-worthy, Kiedis lyrics were infinitely more insightful. Frusciante's guitar melody towards the end of 'Easily' conclusion is nothing short of elegiac. One of their most laidback and pared down moments to date, 'Porcelain' was somnambulist in tone – barely awake. Yet it worked, as some sort of Californian beach-fire torch song, the type of gentle throwaway song Brian Wilson might have penned in the Beach Boys earlier days.

The catchy 'Emit Remmus' concerned a love affair played out in the hot crowded streets of London in summertime – from the Thames river on to Leicester Square then up to Primrose Hill – the title no great puzzle: it was like 'Summer Time' backwards. 'I Like Dirt' was more snappy funk to appeal again to the old school fans who had stuck with the band. Jerky and rocking enough to have not been out on place on *Freaky Styley*, the influence of George Clinton loomed large on this song, the soul of Hillel Slovak somewhere deep in the mix. Another post-addiction song, 'This Velvet Glove' was more of Kiedis as cleaned-up modern-man, the wistful frontman.

'Savior' was all about Frusciante, his howling guitar emoting twisted riffs before the song slips into a trippy, Sixties-style harmonised middle section. It's all a little too standard Chili Peppers though to truly shine though. Of course, the new-found maturity wouldn't last. There was still something very much of the boy's locker room about them and 'Purple Stain' was a bawdy, low-brown funk account of sex with a girl while she's menstruating, leaving nothing to the imagination. Shame – the songs dumb lyrics let down an otherwise strong track. 'Right On Time' was shouty, throwaway funk with a bass beat that unusually for Flea brought nothing new to the record, instead merely labouring the point that the band still had spunk. Worthwhile, but not memorable.

Californication ended on a high note. 'Road Trippin'' was another surprising departure in keeping with the album's clear leap into new modes of expression and new musical territories. With just an acoustic guitar and Kiedis' voice the song is a whimsical song about a trip up the Cali coast, taking in the dramatic Big Sur. The video matched perfectly for this release as a single: another Jonathan Dayton and Valerie Faris production, a very different concept from 'Californication,' and only released in Europe. The band had decamped to Malibu to the borrowed house of an architect friend in order to write a simple acoustic song for the album. The directors followed their progress, making a performance video of the guys sat before the fire strumming acoustic guitar and bass. Intercut into this were images of the band surfing and pulling boats up out of the ocean, running dogs on the beach and building sculptures from kelp and driftwood. It's a different image for the band, showing a softer side to their character. This was perfectly encapsulated by both this future video and the use of a chamber-sounding string section on the track's debut on the album, which brought an air of cultured refinement to a song enlivened by Frusciante's picking. A beautiful close to a remarkable long player.

The album was a complete artistic success, a lively, diverse and emotionally-charged collection. From the striking cover to the melodies within, the Chili's seventh album was infused with the history of California, the dark and light of life at the edge of America. "It's here that the Chili Peppers grow into themselves, and start to trust their ability to write *songs* rather than just *play* music," noted *Kerrang!* The only complaint could have been that, at fifteen songs and nearly an hour long, the album trailed off towards the end in haze of indifferent mellow pop songs. But that was nit-picking. It was an incredibly strong album and The Red Hot Chili Peppers had bounced back from the brink in style.

The modest start to the album's launch belied what would become one of the biggest records of the year and an unconditional and critically lauded return to form for the band perennially on the edge, the Chili Peppers. *Californication* went on to sell six million copies in the US alone, thirteen million worldwide – a massive amount by any artist's standards, not least a band that only months earlier had been drinking at the last chance saloon. The Grammy award they captured was testament to the Chili Pepper's self-belief, and their sense of justification in working through periods of desolate loss and personal pain: punks at heart, they were now millionaires at the bank. A band that should probably have been dead might have hoped to make a good album that would put their stalled career and dodgy sales patterns back on track. Against the odds, the Red Hot Chili Peppers were reborn again. After the torpor of the Navarro years and the rapid ascendancy back to health and sanity – and amazing playing – of John Frusciante, they still had a career. When the guitarist had been adrift in LA, smoking crack, shooting smack and guzzling wine, his teeth reduced to stumps, few could have imagined he would return to assert himself as one of the best guitarists of his generation. It was surely one of the comebacks of the decade.

And yet, once again, it was a record almost completely at odds with the prevailing musical environment of the time. Red Hot Chili Peppers seem to be the band that are *never* actually in fashion. Even way back when funk-rock was fleetingly popular, it was almost as an oddball phenomenon and one that was destined to implode very quickly. Then, when grunge arrived to sweep the world up in its slacker culture and thrift store clothing, the Chilis were very much accepted by the festival-going, long short-wearing fan base. Yet, once again, closer inspection of the music and their image, as well as their lyrical content, reveals that the Chilis were very much the odd ones out at the Seattle-based party.

So it was again here in 1999, when pop ruled the world and sales figures for rock acts were at a real low. The top selling US singles artists of 1999 read like some ghastly nightmare: R Kelly and Celine Dion (*together* no less), Brandy, Britney, Monica, Cher, Ricky Martin, Jennifer Lopez and Will Smith. Of these, Britney Spears had arrived to easily claim the pop princess crown with a debut album that shifted over *twenty million* copies. The Backstreet Boys and N-Sync were still selling shocking amounts – the latter's *No Strings Attached* still holds the world record for being the fastest selling record ever, with an incredible 2.8 million copies sold in the first week alone. There were isolated beacons of hope – an emergent Eminem was already ruffling feathers, Lauryn Hill released a stunning solo album and Limp Bizkit were busy. But for every Fred Durst there was a Westlife – who enjoyed their seventh chart-topping single in the UK. As if Pop Hell itself had arrived, this latest 'smash' was with... Mariah Carey.

So where on earth did the Red Hot Chili Peppers fit into all this? They were old enough to be Britney's parents, seasoned enough to talk of influences that such pop acts had never heard of, and visually and musically at odds with almost every other artist – acclaimed or otherwise – in the charts worldwide. Yet somehow, none of this seemed to matter. Fans bought the record in droves. The Chilis were back and – given the choices at the local record store in this pop-saturated year – thank God for that.

Such was the success of this album that suddenly, Red Hot Chili Peppers were faced with a dilemma that only a few months previously would have seemed unthinkable. They had produced a world-wide best-selling album from the depths of despair, and found themselves on the front pages of not only the music press but the popular media-rags of the world – it was indeed a remarkable achievement, but could it be topped?

CHAPTER 18

The 1999 Woodstock Festival at Griffiths Air Force Base, NY, was a night to remember for many different reasons, not least another naked appearance by Flea. But Woodstock 1999 remains in the memory mainly for the fires that were lit in the crowd during the Chili Pepper's closing set. If the band were smoking, that was nothing compared to the pyres that were set alight by fans as they played: sleeping mats, discarded rubbish and any other items to hand were slung onto the fires, and soon the event was on the edge of chaos. Yet the bill had seemed to offer a sufficiently varied line-up to cater for the musical needs those 225,000 people setting up camp to watch turns from the likes Aerosmith, Korn, Fatboy Slim, Counting Crows, Rage Against The Machine and Willie Nelson.

Over the course of the day the crowd had become more and more restless. From the major label nature of the bands on the bill, the inflated food and drink prices ($12 a pizza, $4 a small bottle of water), and the appearance of cash machines on site, the discovery of which in a field is guaranteed to spoil any acid tripper's high. Even an appearance by master of ceremonies, Wavy Gravy, merely served to remind everyone that the hippy ideal was a relic of the past. Exorbitant prices were being charged for most simple things made worse by stories of people even taking water off kids as they came onto the festival site. Increasingly ill at ease, the crowd had started to voice its collective anger. The band explained that they hadn't realised there was a serious problem: at smaller outdoor gigs, such as on Lollapalooza dates, the fans often lit fires in the crowd. The band saw the fires at Woodstock, but thought little of it. Once again – although they weren't at all implicated in the 'riot' – the Red Hot Chili Peppers saw controversy surround their live performances. As state troopers flooded in alongside members of the fire department, seven arrests were made and five people injured. It could have been a lot worse, but the few 'rioters' caused major headlines in the international press the following day. Anthony told of how he had headed to his home in Manhattan, made some phone calls and went to sleep. When he awoke he found the story all over the papers. It should be pointed out that the crowd violence was equally out of control during sets by both Limp Bizkit and Rage Against The Machine. By the close of the weekend there had been one death, three weddings, thirty-eight arrests (with more to follow), three thousand injuries, fiver trailers destroyed in arson attacks and a lot of exposed breasts, at a total cost of $38 million.

RED HOT CHILI PEPPERS

Despite the chaos of Woodstock 1999, the Peppers themselves were, of course, a cleaner, more sober unit than ever before. Flea was enjoying a domestic life much improved from his days when he would smoke weed all day long. Divorced, but on good terms with his ex-wife who lived nearby, he enjoyed a generous joint-custody arrangement in the care of his daughter Clara, an increasingly intelligent, witty girl who lovingly called her father "the spoilt child" in their relationship, and who had helped him through the exorcism of many of his own personal demons.

On the *Californication* tour, tisanes and incense sticks took the place of narcotics and alcohol backstage. The essence of the massive jaunt was captured on video for the Warner release *Off The Map* (2001). The footage included the obvious crowd-pleasing favourites such as 'Under The Bridge' and 'Californication,' alongside covers of Public Enemy and George Clinton tracks. John performed 'Just A T Shirt,' and the DVD version included almost an hour of backstage and interview footage. However, the film failed to really show the muscle of the band on stage.

Though still capable of getting in one another's hair, the individual members of the band were now more at ease with each another than ever before, able to live independent lives on the road. Flea told *Rolling Stone* that on a night off from the tour he would stay in his room and meditate; Chad would go to strip clubs and get drunk; John would do yoga and play guitar. Flea didn't even say into what Anthony would do! The tour included Russia, the first time that the band had played there. A reputed 300,000 fans crammed into Red Square for the MTV free concert there, despite a mere 90,000 being expected – if those figures were true that would make this show easily one of the biggest concerts for a single act of all-time.

The band found Russia a difficult place to understand: although Flea put himself about a bit and explored Moscow, John failed to leave his hotel room for anything other than his time on stage. Days later the band played Paris, and then onto the UK for Reading and Leeds festivals, where Kiedis said that, "playing Reading was a gas. Being cold and wet in Leeds? I dunno…" Cold and wet they may have been, but by November the band was back in the UK to play at Wembley Arena, supported by Feeder. Long gone were the days when the UK was one of their weakest markets. Now they occupied playlists of all the major radio stations, their concerts were immediate sell-outs on the arena tour circuit and any words uttered by any of the band would guarantee them a front cover feature. Red Hot Chili Peppers were, it seemed, finally in a love/love relationship with the UK.

August 1999 saw a new book in stores across the globe. James Slovak, Hillel's film-editor brother, edited and self-published his brother's diaries. After Hillel's death, James had collected various notebooks and paintings from his apartment and reproduced both Hillel's own handwritten notes and printed text of the same to help readers through Hillel's untidy scrawl. His former band mates contributed too, to a book that gave some insight into Hillel's creativity and mindset, but which disappointed many by its brevity! James wrote touchingly about his brother in the foreword to the book, of how he and his family had known virtually nothing of Hillel's addiction until it was virtually too late. James Slovak clearly loved his brother, as had all his friends in music. A decade and more since his death, he still touched the hearts of those who came across his spirit.

In March 2000, the Peppers were back on the road sporting Mohawk haircuts, with a major tour opening in Minneapolis. No sock-wearing stunts, fire-breathing hats or light bulb costumes on this trip, the band was more relaxed than ever. Chad even joked that for 100 million bucks they'd get the socks back on again! The tour was to be shared with Dave Grohl's Foo Fighters, the post-Nirvana outfit that, while never reaching the ecstatic heights of Grohl's former band in terms of media publicity were nevertheless developing a major international and critical following. On the back of their own album *There is Nothing Left to Lose*, Grohl's band was a natural choice. "Who (else) are we gonna play with," Flea told reporters. "...some rap-metal band, a Korn Jnr?" Flea told the press how the Chili Peppers were on a roll, and expected to be back in the studio immediately after the tour to work on the next album. "We're definitely better than we've ever been," he told reporters. He and Frusciante were experimenting with samplers, and Flea was carrying a four-track recorder with him on tour, hoping to include some of his compositions on the next Chili Peppers' album, even discussing the possibility of making a solo outing.

Anthony, meanwhile, was happily settled in with Yohanna, his girlfriend of more than a year, living together near to LA's Sunset Boulevard. Kiedis even told interviewers how he felt near to settling down and having a family with her. Yohanna joined Kiedis on the tour occasionally, spending time in Bali and Hawaii between dates.

The tour was another massive onslaught for the band, working through Wisconsin, Illinois, Ohio, New York State and well into the month of May. *Melody Maker* caught up with the band in Australia, playing the Big Day Out festival, with Joe Strummer, Primal Scream and the Foo Fighters in attendance. It was a scorching schedule, but during the year Flea also managed to fit in work on the score of the Steven Soderbergh movie *Traffic*. The film, starring Hollywood darlings Michael Douglas and Catherine Zeta Jones, was a tense thriller: its soundtrack was a soothing, intelligent and ambient affair scored by early-Chili Pepper Cliff Martinez, and featured Flea and Herbie Hancock on some tracks, with Fatboy Slim, Morcheeba and Brian Eno also contributing.

Kiedis was busy with a side project of his own. Anthony has often been keen to talk about his own loves – family, friendships, his own survival against the odds in the hectic world of rock and roll. It is almost as if by discussing these issues openly and in public he continues to shore up his own inner strength and keep the demons at bay. But not just a show-biz charity face, Kiedis was increasingly involved in helping the homeless around Los Angeles (he and Flea also famously catwalked for a Jean-Paul Gaultier charity show to benefit AIDS research in 1992). In December he helped with a late Thanksgiving meal in aid of the charity for homeless kids called Stand Up For Kids.

Late in October, the Chili Peppers joined the Dave Matthews Band, Tom Petty, Beck and the Foo Fighters at Neil Young's annual charity gig the Bridge School Benefit concert. It was an emotionally charged date, a downpour of rain for five hours of the eight-hour event lending it, somehow, more atmosphere. The two-day gig was in its fourteenth year: fourteen years of raising funds for the disabled children who attended the school; fourteen years of ego-reduced rock star benevolence. After blistering sets from the other bands, the Chili Peppers took the stage and sounded better than ever, more like an excited greasy back-room bar band than an outfit with twenty years history and the scars to show for them. They included two covers in a set of favourites – 'Beverly Hills' by the Circle Jerks and Cat Stevens' 'Trouble,' a restrained set-closer. Chad Smith tossed drum sticks to the gaggle of kids from the school lined up back stage, and as the evening drew to a close, Flea joined the re-formed Crosby, Stills, Nash and Young (along with actor Woody Harrelson) for a resplendent rendition of the pop classic 'Love The One You're With'.

At the inaugural 2000 VH-1 Awards in November, Flea confirmed that the Peppers were ready to hit the studio again to begin work on the much-anticipated follow-up to *Californication*. The awards ceremony was a major event, broadcast live on TV and the internet, with viewers able to vote online as the ceremony progressed. Flea mentioned that while the band had not lined up a producer, it was pretty likely that Rick Rubin would be on board once more. The band was clearly comfortable in their skin again with touring and recording dates jigsawing into one another comfortably. The magic, for Flea, was in not planning too much and following their instinct. Once the process of a tour was completed, the process of putting together the next album would follow without too much pre-conception.

Kiedis too spoke of how music was a self-perpetuating addiction, a drug that both supplied the highs and healed itself. "I love pot, and I love beer," he told *Interview* magazine, "but music is a built-in lubricant to create itself. Once you start playing... you become even more creative." This was a band who had worked through many demons to get where they were today, and as their music became more simple, more pop-orientated and more song-led than groove-led, it was their maturity as self-knowing adults, that made it stand out from all the other bands around them.

Their benevolent work did not stop there. Early in 2001, it was announced that the band would play with Neil Young and Thelonious Monster at the Hollywood Palladium in aid of the musicians'charity MAP. The Musicians Assistance Program helps people in the music industry to deal with addiction and substance abuse issues, and this was a return favour from Young for the Chili Peppers' own appearance at his Bridge School benefit the previous year. Tickets for the March 1st show went on sale in February, with VIP seats priced at $150 apiece. Anthony was also indebted to MAP's Gloria Scott, who supported him during some of the darkest days of his addictions, and who is remembered on the song 'Venice Queen'.

By April, rumours that Flea would be playing live with Jane's Addiction on their Fall reunion tour were being hotly denied. The Chili Peppers were still working on the follow-up to *Californication*, and fans worried that this might be one side-project too many. In the meantime however, evidence of some of Frusciante and Kiedis' free time was released, as Tricky – trip hopper-fantastique of the Nineties – released his first album on Hollywood Records. The album featured John and Anthony on the fourth track 'Girls', a light amalgam of Tricky's new rap style and Chili Peppers' groove. For many the album was a mystery, given the superb debut of Tricky's *Maxinquaye*, while for others it was a return to form following earlier lesser records. What typified many reviewers' responses, however, was a failure to understand the presence of John and Anthony at all...

August saw the band in the UK once again, headlining the huge V2001 festivals in Essex and Staffordshire. Britain was in the grip of foot and mouth fever, with the fear of the killer disease causing even more havoc amongst the nation's farmers. Movement in agricultural areas of the country had been severely restricted, tens of thousands of livestock slaughtered, but the expectation was that the long hot summer would help reduce the threat of the disease. Alongside the Chili Peppers, Coldplay, Doves, Grandaddy Toploader, and many other top bands were lined up for the event. Flea, Kiedis and Co took the stage late in the evening, headlining both nights' bills. Opening up the band's set, Frusciante hit the stage alone, sporting a fetching woolly hat and tearing strips off of his guitar for half a minute before the rest of the band joined him. They ripped into 'Give It Away' (via a little PiL), 'Scar Tissue' and 'Higher Ground,' – a welcome dip into *Mother's Milk* for the die-hard fans who had braved a healthy dose of English summer rain. The years of jamming together and working through their long-lasting friendship showed when Frusciante's amp blew in mid-song. Flea, Smith and Kiedis hammed-up an improvisatory jam until the problem was sorted out by a rash of wet roadies who scuttled around the stage, and they were back on course for a memorable evening.

In true Chilis style, it wasn't all sweetness and light though: while the band were engaged elsewhere Flea had a pile of music gear stolen from a storage locker in Los Angeles over the summer months, losing instruments and mementos from his career to date. Later in the month, the former bad boys of funk joined the rather more establishment likes of Sting and Elton John at the nevertheless worthy Silver Lining Silver Lake Benefit concert. In aid of the Hollywood Sunset Free Clinic, and sharing the three-day bill with Aimee Mann, the band played a forty-five minute set including 'Don't Forget', 'Universally Speaking' and 'Fortune Faded' – new tracks from the forthcoming album.

Silver Lake is a creative community a few miles to the north west of downtown Los Angeles, the site of many early film studios such as Mack Sennett's and Disney. Many of the Keystone Cops car chases were filmed on the streets of Silver Lake, while the Chili Peppers and many other contemporary artists lived within easy reach of the area. It was here that Flea became involved in the Silverlake Conservatory of Music, which opened its doors for the first time in October. Flea had performed a benefit gig at his own former school, and was shocked by the lack of musical resources there and in mainstream education in general. Intent on finding a way to allow young school kids to find a route to music outside of the plastic and glossy world of MTV, he hooked up with a former school-friend and music teacher by the name of Keith Barry. Flea was – if you can excuse the pun – instrumental in funding the Conservatory, even planning to give trumpet and bass lessons there himself. The former thrift store boasted eight practice rooms, and it was Flea's intent that alongside Haydn and Bartok, students would study punk rock, Afro-Cuban music and other contemporary forms. The school also hoped that the other Chili Peppers might offer some time for teaching there too, but recognised that Flea's commitment to his band must come first, and that he would probably offer two-month slots for teaching between Chili Pepper work.

Kept busy by live gigs here and there, the band had most of the instrumental tracks for the next studio album down already, while Kiedis was busy writing lyrics. "I've pretty much done all my contributions," Flea told journalists, while Kiedis predicted that shows in the future would be loaded up with new material: "...we're so happy with the songs we wrote."

In March, Kiedis spoke about the new album, and the changes in the band that fans could expect on the forthcoming release. Frusciante would play keyboards as well as guitars, and Anthony's own lyrics would explore with more sensitivity the break of up of the three-year relationship with girlfriend Yohanna that had just come to an end. "I've never felt comfortable writing 'love songs,'" said Kiedis, "or 'relationship songs,' but it's sneaking in there..." The couple split when Kiedis reached the point where he wanted to start a family. Yohanna wasn't ready to go that far, and the relationship foundered. Anthony told a journalist from *Guitar Magazine* that "a lot of it is about either being in love or the desire to be in love. It's definitely what I have been feeling for the last year. A profound sense of wanting love in my daily life." Anthony had been heartbroken at the split with Yohanna, unhappy and lonely. No surprise then that he sought love in his life and in his music.

CHAPTER 19

The Chili Peppers were clearly refreshed and renewed for the follow-up to *Californication*. Yet even their most ardent fans would be pushed to call the Red Hot Chili Peppers of yore sophisticated. Accomplished, yes. Talented, imaginative and energetic too, but never sophisticated. Wearing nothing but socks on cocks and singing about booty can do that to a band.

Yet with this eighth album, to be called *By The Way*, they achieved what had seemed unachievable. Everything came together perfectly. The hard knocks, tragedies, addictions and hard partying had been enforced exercises in life affirmation and as the band approached forty they were irrevocably older, but infinitely wiser with it. *By The Way* saw the Red Hot Chili Peppers finally shrugging off the funk-rock shackles and freeing themselves from the slavish devotion to all things irreverent, cartoon-ish. It was no sudden about turn though, as *Californication* had ably displayed. But its success had given them more confidence to make a multi-textured rock record. Not a party on plastic like *Freaky Styley*, but something far more lasting.

Finally all drug–free in the studio – Flea had given up his habit of smoking vast amounts of weed every day – the Chilis developed their new found clarity. In came Mellotrons, Beach Boys harmonies and softly-woven melodies, and as the last vestiges of rap-rock dissipated, Kiedis discovered he could *sing*. Using Pro Tools, the favoured software of the contemporary recording studio, to add vocal tracks to the instrumentals laid down previously, they set up on the seventh floor at the Chateau Marmont hotel on Sunset Boulevard ("in the back, where it's a little less noisy," said Anthony). Kiedis told the story of how he only had one comment from a fellow guest, a British novelist working in the next room, who found that his wailing and screaming inspired her to work better herself. Typical Anthony, his major moan was that this was the only time they met!

His vocals were all recorded in that seventh floor suite and as a result carried a new-found warmth to complement Frusciante, who was running at his very best. Chad told *Interview* magazine that a lot of the credit for the forthcoming success of *By The Way* must go to Frusciante. "He'd come to rehearsal and show up ready," he said. "John would have the record written in half an hour… and I think it brought everyone up a level." What so distinguished the sound of *By The Way* was the immense care and effort taken by Frusciante in particular, layering countless overdubs onto the basic tracks: background vocals; guitars; synthesizers and more. Filling the album with harmonies and more rich, creative sounds than ever before, Frusciante's contribution was all over the finished piece, but nowhere more evident than on 'The Zephyr Song', 'Dosed' and 'I Could Die For You'. The same level of care was evident in the clip for 'Zephyr Song', the second single from the album. This was to become one of the band's most enduring videos. Retro-styled – the clip is very much an affectionate pastiche of Sixties psychedelia – the video took six weeks of editing images of dancers and band. The abiding image is based upon the kind of 'folded-over' ink-blots used in psychological diagnosis. The languorous guitar opening of 'Zephyr Song' is matched in the Dayton/Faris video by the sinuous dancing of the woman chosen from the many strip-joint and nightclub dancers who auditioned for the part. None of them seemed to bring the kind of style to the show that the band and directors wanted, until at last they found their girl. Band and dancer are blended in endless, superimposed psychedelic images, paying homage to but not trying to ape the era of the Pink Floyd light show and 1970s disco.

Frusciante had himself been continuously honing his guitar technique, learning style after style: individual guitar greats like Bert Jansch and Johnny Marr, British guitar pickers of the first order from the Sixties and Eighties respectively. He told The Toronto Sun that he had learned all the songs from The Smiths' catalogue, and was studying another English guitar master, Richard Thompson, late of Fairport Convention and, for many, 'the guitarist's guitarist.' Alongside this he took much from the recordings of Siouxie and The Banshees and fellow new-wavers Magazine, and the guitar work of John McGeoch who – as well as these bands – graced the work of Public Image Ltd, Generation X and The Armoury Show. McGeoch's death in March 2004 received broad coverage in the general press worldwide, not just in the music mags, and testified to his quiet influence across two decades of guitar pop. Other name-checks from John included Vinny Reilly of the British band Durrutti Column and Andy Partridge, the leading light behind post-punksters XTC, whose mature work right through to the twenty-first century has been wonderful.

As on *Californication*, John's guitar style leaned more towards the sound-textures and atmospheres that his instrument could create rather than sizzling mechanical technique. "I'm much more influenced by Kraftwerk than by guitarists' solos," he told Total Guitar Magazine.

"When I hadn't played guitar in five years I could pick (one up) anytime and play that kind of flashy stuff, and I hadn't been practising at all. But there was no feeling there." Frusciante's years in narcotic hell had cleared out the self-revering element of the rock guitar soloist from his make-up. Over the years, the kind of solo playing to which John referred – extended, twenty-minute workouts from some guy with his face screwed up like a wet washing-up rag – had kind of run their course. Hundreds of metal and glam-metal bands kept the tradition alive of course, and a million or more air guitarists across America would always cry out for more, but for Frusciante this was a thing of the past. He still admired the likes of Eric Clapton and, of course, Hendrix, but saw in the work of the guitarists of the late Seventies and Eighties ideas that were overlooked in favour of incendiary firebombs from the Eddie van Halen school of rock. "I don't feel that's the way for guitar playing to continue," he said. The key was to think outside of blues traditions, traditions that kept the guitarist on a particular scale and kept his fingers running through the same series' of notes every time he hit a solo: "It's good knowing that you're looking at the guitar in ways that it's not been looked at before."

For guitar junkies who want to know what equipment Frusciante used on the album, here's a quick run through... Effect pedals were used in moderation, but John likes the older models like the Big Muff, a rich, creamy sustain pedal that has distorted the guitar of Carlos Santana for many a year. Those ethereal, sweeping sounds come from an Electro-Harmonix flanger, filtering the guitar spectrum to produce beautiful effects. John used his favoured Ibanez WH10 wah-wah pedal on 'Don't Forget Me,' but less across the whole album than previously, and he favours old amplifiers too, using 1960s Fender equipment alongside modern synthesizers to get fantastic reverb. The album featured a lot of volume-pedal work too, to get that gentle guitar sound on 'Don't Forget About Me.' On most of the songs John used a 1962 Fender Stratocaster (he had used a '58 model on Californication), with Gibson SGs, a Fender Jazzmaster and Gretsches here and there.

Flea also refined his technique and changed his style of playing for the album to a degree. Forced to develop his technique with the guitar pick instead of with his well-honed thumb so that he could play with Jane's Addiction, Flea found himself using the pick at jams with his own band. The difference a pick makes is to inject more attack into the note played:

a note played with the thumb will have a thicker, chunkier sound to it – traditionally a 'funkier' sound. A note played with the pick will be harder, more precise. Flea found the chord structures that John brought to the sessions ideal for his new-found interest, and developed a more melodic approach through the change in style. The melodic approach was also inspired by Paul McCartney. Flea told Bass Player magazine that where most Chili Peppers songs were born off a bass riff and built up from there, he had read that The Beatles' bass player always laid his tracks down last. Throughout his long career the often-underrated bassist McCartney has rarely faltered in this department, and Flea took the idea to heart, re-doing his fretless bass track on "I Could Die For You" over the top of the existing tracks.

John was typically modest when he was asked about his own contribution to the album. While the other members of the band told the worlds' press that this was much more 'his' album – filled with his writing, arrangements and overdubs – Frusciante was quick to point out that as far as he was concerned it was as much a band effort as ever. He was clearly able to write with a defined purpose now. On the subject of his drug use, he pointed out that when they recorded *Bloodsugarsexmagic* he and Flea were doing a lot of weed but that Anthony wasn't: "My recommendation to musicians is you all smoke pot or none of you do." On the new album the band was clean and together in the sense that they all shared much the same head-space.

Back to the album itself, the opening song and title track 'By The Way' unveiled the sophisticated new-millennial Chilis with aplomb. With a brooding backbeat, angular riffing and a chorus designed for the radio airwaves, it set a high standard for the album, the perfection transition from *Californication*'s sun-drenched introspection. With a suitably dramatic video, it became another huge hit. Dayton and Faris produced another memorable video clip for 'By The Way,' a mini-movie in which Anthony is kidnapped by a crazy taxi driver (Dave Sheridan) and rescued by Flea and Chad. At the beginning Anthony hails the cab – holding up a book about his favourite punk band The Germs! – but as the driver recognises him, and slips a Chili Peppers disk into his CD player, it all starts to go wrong. Intercut with fantastic live footage of the band, the comical Starsky & Hutch-style car chase comes to a conclusion after Anthony texts his mates from the back of the cab. They pull alongside the taxi in downtown traffic, and in a move that Indiana Jones would have been proud of, Anthony leaps from one vehicle to the other in mid-highway. Apparently, although a stuntman was booked to do the leap, the work is Anthony's own.

It became the opening single for the new album campaign: a snapshot of LA night- life, from hookers to dealers, gambling to car crashes. The old-fashioned vocoder vocal effect lifts the track, the guitars and driving bass pushing the track onwards, bringing together many of the things that had brought the band to this point: funk, rock, passion, mixed down with keen observation. This was one of the few tracks on the album to remind listeners of the old Peppers, with the rest of the album concentrating more on subtlety and mood than power and energy.

The delicate, shimmering 'Universally Speaking' may have initially came across as Motown-lite, but was actually a crafty pop song that was the Chili Peppers' closest Beach Boys moment and Kiedis' most confident vocal workout to date. Whether Chad Smith got the urge to beat the hell of the gentle, unwavering drum backbeat is not known, but such temperance and fastidiousness in the album was typical of the album. Frusciante in particular pored over takes, tweaking his parts as Rick Rubin captured the sound.

'This Is The Place' saw the same sense of more moody sophistication the band had exuded to great effect on their quietly elegant crossover hit 'Under The Bridge'. An understated work of beauty, 'Dosed' was a showcase for Kiedis previously-untapped falsetto singing voice, Frusciante's guitars chiming delicately on a work that recalled the melodies of accomplished songwriters like Cat Stevens and the lush production of Phil Spector... if they had recorded in hotel rooms. It was something of a self-effacing creative high for the band and approximately one million miles away from 'Skinny Sweaty Man'.

For John Frusciante, *Californication* was about him affirming himself at the top as the guitar work. On 'Don't Forget Me', a song whose lyrics hinted at Kiedis, he suggested his days of heroin were well and truly behind him. 'The Zephyr Song' began with the sound of the Red Hot Chili Peppers first flirtation with electronica to date and was, in terms of dynamics, rather weak. Yet, in its fairy-tale-like chorus and fantastical lyrics lay enough guitar-pop hooks to ensure it was to become another successful single.

From its juddering, portentous opening, 'Can't Stop' was the best song on the album, another career high point. That it was a funk-rap song at its very best suggested the Chilis could never fully relinquish their past because it was a past worth revisiting. With one of the spikiest guitar riffs ever heard driving it Kiedis' closely-miked rap layered over the top it was a song played directly from the groin; *but,* crucially, smart as opposed to smut. They still had the funk alright, but this time they finally knew how to use it to their best advantage. Interestingly, the video for this track on its single release was the band's most surreal to date: directed by Mark Romanek, it was a superb distillation onto film of the 'one minute sculptures' of artist Erwin Wurm. Wurm encourages ordinary, non-artist people to engage in short performances with everyday objects, thus creating their own individual works of art. Romanek worked the band very hard – the video was as arduous in its filming as any performance video. The result was a graphically intriguing collection of images: Anthony bellowing into a long yellow tube, or standing within the bricks of a wall that contains an Anthony-shaped hole; Flea suspended from the ceiling; John playing his guitar on top of an office chair. The band members become part of the artworks themselves, but Romanek maintained an element of fun throughout the whole piece – it's not too far removed from clips from the 1960's *Monkees* TV series, and remains one of the band's favourite videos.

The string-laden 'I Could Die For You' was earnest to an extreme in its declaration of love and dedication, though the Beatles-esque chorus redeemed the song from being too much of a saccharine-sweet overload. Previous albums had tended to see the band trail off somewhere in the second half and *By The Way* was no exception – a song like the harmony-laden 'Midnight' was just too mundane to be interesting, too blatant to matter. Fans from the late Eighties era would surely have been wringing their socks in anguish. In their favour, the Chili Peppers were finally confident enough to experiment much more with sound and flit between styles. The clumsily-titled 'Throw Away Your Television' was pretty much a bass-led jam with a disco-sounding middle section, one idea stretched to breaking point. If *By The Way* could have benefited from being shorter, then this was surely the first song the band could have left in the archives.

'Cabron' – meaning 'brother' – was the flipside of this musical confidence. A percussive mariachi stomp with a melody to die for it was another departure for the band yet a completely natural one, Frusciante's deft picking and Kiedis' believable crooning stamping the band's sound on a song they would once have never dreamed of attempting; it almost sounded like a Hawaii-era Elvis off-cut. In this case, it was no bad thing. 'Tear' was another languid ballad, largely forgettable save for an epic chorus for those who like to wave lighters at concerts. That and the fact that Flea put his refined trumpet skills to use once again.

'On Mercury' was one of the band's few attempts at recording a ska song– surprising, given the music's close proximity to punk, funk and reggae. But even more strangely, it worked. Sounding like it had just skanked up from south of the border, it was the sound of a band still partying, just not as hard as before and without the aid of opiates (given the west coat's love affair with ska, particularly the so-called third-wave of that genre which saw bands such as No Doubt and the Mighty Mighty Bosstones enjoy massive success, it was indeed surprising that the Chilis had never tried this venture before). 'Minor Thing' was an unassuming song; the type of lasting low-key rock song you realise you really like only after listening to the album for six months. It was worth hearing for Frusciante's Ennio Morricone-inspired guitar solo. With haunting, warping keyboard sounds and ill-fitting lyrics 'Warm Tape' was easily *By The Way*'s most experimental, esoteric song. It worked, but brought nothing new to an otherwise strong set of songs. Ethereal album closer 'Venice Queen' was dedicated to Anthony's drug counsellor and the lyrics certainly read like a thank-you note to someone, Frusciante again nimbly lifting the song into a world of its own.

Critics were quick to point out the fact that the band that had made *By The Way* had a combined age of 150 – only it wasn't necessarily a complaint. Most people were just surprised the all-new mature Red Hot Chili Peppers as heard on *Californication* hadn't been a fluke. That they had returned with an even stronger album was commendable. And even if it was their most gentle offering yet, it was also their most diverse. Simply put, if the band had carried on making funk-rock records they would have been long gone.

This was an issue the band was clearly aware of. Interviews referred to the influence of California voices of the past such as Cass Elliot from the Mamas & The Papas. Chad Smith agreed, with the admission that the band's anthemic, stadium style was ready for a change: "To me it's like, we've done the fist-pumping funk songs and did it great... you can't keep doing the same thing. You have to change. It's more difficult to write a simple, melodic song!" Although Kiedis claimed not to listen to contemporary music for fear of it creeping into the band's sound, it was clear that Rick Rubin's record collection had had a major influence, with great records of the past such as The Seekers' 'Georgy Girl' and any number of Beatles' tracks being amongst those cited. John claimed to have studied anything he could that contained harmony, in love with the blended voices of great pop from the past.

Once again, almost as if it was a prerequisite of any successful Chili Peppers album, their sound and look were not particularly in keeping with the alternative bands that were selling records during this time, most notably the Strokes and the White Stripes. The former New York foursome had found great favour with both a fawning music press and an excitable fashion cogniscenti, with their clever and direct blend of Velvet Underground pastiche and modernist delivery. They were a brilliant, breath-taking and refreshing band, despite wearing their influences so clearly on their sleeve. In their wake, a thousand and one leather-clad Strokes wannabe bands sprang up, almost to the point of caricature, but the New York foursome remained the original and best. Same with Detroit's The White Stripes – a duo of drums and guitar only, led by the enigmatic Jack White and his former wife Meg. They celebrated Detroit's garage rock history and fused it seamlessly with the blues to create a fantastic yet brutally simple combination. In both cases, music-lovers were smitten. Of course, hardly any single element of these two bands bore much resemblance to what the Chilis were doing. There was no funk in Jack White's Robert Johnson-esque guitar; there was no Lou Reed in Flea's staggering bass lines. Rock historians would no doubt thread some of these influences into the Chilis in some way, but the fact is, once again they flew in the face of the prevailing music fashion. And once again, it simply didn't matter.

The cover artwork for *By The Way*, by acclaimed New York-based neo-expressionist artist Julian Schnabel, was an eye-catching oil painting of a naked women seen from the waist up, set against a photographic background, the band's askew name framing it in red and blue painting. It was actually of his daughter Stella, who was dating Frusciante and the band call Schnabel father-in-law. He was so impressed by the album that he could sing the songs down the phone to Kiedis from memory.

By The Way was not without its problems. For a while it seemed that the album would never be released. Originally scheduled for a June release, it was held back while the band continued working on it. "It's going to spank your ass," said Kiedis at one awards ceremony. "We have enough to be done and finished, but instead we just keep going further. Just because we don't stop. We can't stop!" During the making of the record, Kiedis had referred to about thirty songs in interviews, from which the band would choose maybe fifteen for the album release: it was difficult trying to keep some kind of perspective on the album's release with so much quality material available. At sixteen songs and sixty-eight minutes in length, some argued the Chili Peppers may have over-indulged themselves.

The album was a perfect snapshot of contemporary LA. If 'Under The Bridge' had summed up the dark under-belly of the city, its drug culture and airless quality, then the new songs caught the city's poetic side, its bohemian romanticism, ravaged but undeterred. The album blended sophisticated pop arrangements and retro-styling, introspective lyrics and an ever-present sense of the song coming before the performance. The effect of this was to view the city at the heart of popular culture through a series of pop culture filters, a neat trick for a band who themselves had never been limited to one point of view or style.

In May the band convened in a swanky Santa Monica hotel to launch the album to the world's press and to air it in public for the first time. Flea relaxed with some yoga. Kiedis – wearing a little goatee beard – was nervous and quiet. John arrived looking like Jesus of Nazareth, while Chad Smith rolled in last, looking as though he had been dragged out of bed to attend. Nineteen years together, this was only the second time that the band line-up had remained unchanged from one album to the next, and journalists were keen to figure out the secrets of this unusual bunch of guys. Rick Rubin pointed out how Flea in particular had developed from stoned-out nervous jock into an abstinent and well-read, all-round bachelor guy with a thirteen-year-old daughter. Many of the current young bands around were now in fact young enough to be the sons and daughters of the Chili Peppers, but Flea proudly boasted that – with his hair in various shades of blue – he remained an embarrassment to his daughter for being a boring old punk!

Q magazine found Frusciante a contradictory character. Clean of drugs and re-habilitated within the family/band, he nevertheless appeared to have a tenuous grasp on anything beyond his own music. Referring to the events of 9/11, he mentioned the tragedy at the Empire State Building. The magazine touchingly noted that John may well be the only person in America unaware of which building was the target for the terrorists on that day, but concluded that the fact that he was still alive at all was to be celebrated. John spoke of the horrors of his time living the junky life at the Chateau Marmont. John talked of what it had been like to be no longer recognised in public, and of how childhood traumas that he never even remembered had crept up on him. "It's like I'm remembering someone else's life," he said of the days before his collapse. He referred to the 'spirits' who haunted him throughout his illness and addiction, and – still acknowledging their existence – pointed out that all that had changed was that now those spirits liked him.

John has always talked of the 'spiritual' side to his music. For him, music is something that comes to us through the air from somewhere else, it is an invisible thread linking people and places, passed to one individual in a recording studio and then via him to millions of people beyond. In an interview with *Classic Rock* magazine he compared the process to God, and likened the musicians role to that of a latter-day witch. This concept of a muse being a foil through which writers simply picked songs up out of the ether, rather than creating them through their own genius, was one that had been talked about for years, with notable stars expressing some belief in this including Keith Richards and Bob Dylan no less.

By contrast, in the same interview in *Q* magazine, Chad Smith was the perfect 'likeable drummer.' How many bands have had a similar guy behind the skins? So many drummers seem grounded where their band-mates are not. Maybe it's the fact that they sit down when they go to work, like regular office guys?! Maybe it's the genuine hard physical labour of playing the drums – instead of catapulting one's self around the stage in a frenzy of self-regard – that makes them more like builders than wizards and seers? Maybe it's the fact that they spend their careers staring at their band-mate's arses instead of down into the mosh pit at the upturned adoring faces? "It's all smoke and mirrors, my friend," Chad told the magazine, "...there's dark places!"

The punk ethic of the Red Hot Chili Peppers survived well into *By The Way*. If they now drove fast cars and lived in fancy houses, they nevertheless retained a vibrancy and earnestness in what they produced that is at the essence of punk – recall, too, that apart from Frusciante, they had never disowned or shied away from the financial benefits of being a successful rock band. Nor should they.

Going back to 9/11, this catastrophic event had occurred during the making of this record. Surely the softer quality of *By The Way* was in part affected by the events of 9/11, which the band – and the whole world – watched with grief and sadness. As America reeled from the horrors of that day, the Chili Peppers took some of that hopelessness and despair into the studio with them, and although they denied its specific influence, the album is clearly a more reflective set than ever before. Interestingly, the band had been scheduled to play in Israel, and had cancelled the dates a month before 9/11 for security reasons. Kiedis and Frusciante found 9/11 turned their heads around to some of the more beautiful aspects of living in such a scarred age, but also made them think – like everybody else who was moved by the event – of their immediate future. Flea in particular considered moving to Australia (his natural home) where he has a home. Holidaying in St Barts over the previous Christmas break, floating in the blue waters of the Caribbean, they found a beauty to counter the destruction of the assault on New York the previous Fall. Older and wiser, as the band left their teens, twenties and most of their thirties behind them, it was in general a more pensive time. The album reflects the balance between passionate party time and the darker side: "Because of our willingness to keep changing, evolving and growing, and not feeling like we have to keep repeating ourselves, the music is always fresh," Flea told one interviewer. Their fan-base – evolving into an ever-changing and ever-broadening church itself – was ready for the ride. "I think the openness, and the willingness to embrace everything around… is something everyone can relate to," Flea continued. The band seemed generally reflective on disk as well as in interviews at the time – perhaps to some extent just glad to still be alive, never mind making some of the best music of their career some twenty years after their first forays in the business.

On its release in summer 2002, *By The Way* entered the charts at number one on five continents and at least 16 countries, including the UK, Ireland, Holland, Australia and Canada. The video was nominated for the top award in the music industry, the MTV VMA Award. Soon after, *By The Way* went platinum in twenty-six countries and became the biggest selling success of the Red Hot Chili Peppers strange and wonderful career to date.

CHAPTER 20

Rather worryingly for the bands left trailing in this juggernaut album's wake, Kiedis told reporters that he felt the band was only just beginning to fulfil its potential. The Chili Peppers always made progress, no matter what, but it seemed perhaps now that they could go forward on their own terms instead of dodging from crisis to crisis. The fact that it took them eighteen years to finally crack the big, big time with *Californication*, meant that when they truly made it they were adults who had gone through their growing pains, survived their tragedies already, and could respond to success with a measure of perspective.

At the MTV show taped at a skateboard park in Orange County to promote the album, the audience were slow to warm up. Eyes locked together as they are for so many jams, Flea and Frusciante showed how many of their work-outs start, and their re-focused jamming brought the crowd around at last. The band played dates and a launch in Spain, appearing at the Salon de las Columnas del Circulo de Bellas Artes in Madrid, as well as doing TV dates there too. After the gig the band spent time talking to fans, and John in particular was very approachable and chatted for ten minutes or so before heading off.

The 2002 tour promoting *By The Way* was another mammoth affair. Sporting a T-shirt with the legend "Fuck Me I'm Famous," Anthony cut a dash across the stadia of the world, performing again to hundreds of thousands of fans.

In September Flea reportedly paid $30,000 for a painting by the artist Brian Warner. The portrait, of 'Black Dahlia' Elizabeth Short, showed the victim of one of LA's most notorious unexplained crimes. Found murdered and naked in a field over half a century before, the body of Elizabeth had been ceremoniously cut in two. Reuters reported Flea's purchase not so much for the subject matter itself, but for the fact that Warner is of course better known as Marilyn Manson. His exhibit 'The Golden Age of Grotesque' attracted a great deal of attention.

The newly revitalised Frusciante worked on his fourth solo album project in parallel to *By The Way*, this time using real studios instead of recording at home. Perhaps surprisingly, given the accolades showered on him after *By The Way* was released, John revealed that he had been doing other things at the time. "My energies were equally distributed between *By The Way* and this other album," the guitarist told Kieran Grant of *The Toronto Sun*. On a creative roll, he had so much more material than fitted into the Chili Pepper's plans at the time, and he spoke of his non-stop work ethic outside of the day job. "I consider it my responsibility," he told Grant, "to write as many songs as I can and to record as many as I can… it's the reason that I'm living."

John's fourth solo release did not see the light of day until early in 2004. Featuring Bicycle Thief John Klinghoffer alongside Smith and Flea, the album promised a mix of human warmth and clinical yet exhilarating electronica.

In October 2002, Chad was the first Chili Pepper to turn forty years old. Divorced from the mother of his five-year-old daughter, he also now had a daughter of sixteen months, Ava. Chad celebrated his birthday with a 'pimp and ho' party, to which Frusciante came dressed as a giant pimple and Flea came as a garden hoe! From early 2003, EMI re-released remastered versions of the band's first four albums, each with bonus demos, live tracks and other unreleased material. The distance they had travelled from early Parliament and Funkadelic influences to the Beach Boys-influenced eighth album was clear for all to hear. Another mighty tour kicked off in January. The band played night after night after night, seemingly without a break: from the first dates in Portugal they moved through Spain, seeing off Italy before moving through Germany and France. Sell-out gigs in the UK started in Glasgow, and then London and Manchester were polished off before returning to mainland Europe and gigs in Belgium, Switzerland, Germany and Holland (these four all in five days!). Finland, Norway and Sweden closed the European dates in late March, and by May they were ready to re-group and start a twenty-five city heave across the breadth of the North American continent. Mars Volta joined them in Europe, and Queens Of The Stone Age and (later in the tour) Snoop Dogg carried the US tour dates with them after the death of a member of the Mars Volta crew. Summer saw Chili Peppers back in the UK for the V festival dates, and appearances at German festivals too. Back in the USA in September, with French Toast joining the tour instead of Snoop Dogg, the band played right through October.

The tour clearly proved a number of things, should there be anybody left alive who doubted their credentials. Firstly, the Flea/Frusciante/Smith trio is one of the most accomplished and powerful in all of contemporary rock. Without doubt they had reached a point of major achievement, blistering their way through a blend of funk and metal that few bands could emulate. Kiedis repeatedly proved himself a remarkable, committed performer. Capable of gymnastics displays that any Olympic squad would be proud of, and with a voice clearly benefiting from increasing years of abstinence, he had become one of rock's truly charismatic performers. The sight of the quartet bouncing on their toes as they set off into the opening numbers, churning out pop with attitude, wit, and feeling was a sight to behold. Joni Mitchell once remarked that great music should have something for the head to think about, something for the heart to care about and something to make your feet want to dance: The Red Hot Chili Peppers had all three in spades.

As if all this activity wasn't enough it was announced early in 2003 that *Scar Tissue*, the autobiography of Anthony Kiedis would be published by Hyperion Press of New York City. Hot on the heels of a top-selling album and sell-out tour, the publisher certainly expected their author – who would co-write with an established author – to "stand as naked as he has sometimes appeared on stage," as company president Bob Miller put it. At the time of going to press, the book is scheduled for publication in November 2004.

By now, the Chili Peppers were so successful and so revered that there seemed to be no end to the amount of side projects that they were presented with. For example, long time fans of rock icons The Ramones, the Chili Peppers were chosen by Johnny Ramone to cut the lead track on the newly-released tribute album to the leather-clad wonders of comic-book punk released in February. *We're A Happy Family: A Tribute to The Ramones* was a project a long time in the making. Johnny Ramone and White Zombie front-man Rob Zombie handpicked the various contributors, each of whom provided a track for the album. *Rolling Stone* described the collection as "a tribute album that doesn't suck!" The list of contributors included Marilyn Manson, U2, Metallica, The Pretenders, Garbage and Tom Waits – an eclectic choice, and one that paid full tribute to the foursome who were probably the most influential of the New York punk bands of the mid- to late Seventies. Without The Ramones, rock might have plodded on at the pedestrian pre-punk pace of the prog- and glam-rock eras. The Ramones speeded up the pop song, pared down its musicianship to basic guitar, bass and drums, and uniformed rock once and for all with the T-shirt and torn jeans image. The Chili Peppers' track was 'Havana Affair', a track that they played live on regular occasions, and, tucked quietly in at the end of the album, a gem from John Frusciante, 'Today Your Love, Tomorrow The World'.

During a tour of Europe on which they played support to the Ramones back in the Eighties, the Chili Peppers had endeared themselves to their older cousins in a unique and hilarious way. According to biographer Dave Thompson, the bands were appearing in Finland, seven months into a ball-breaking tour, and it was the last night. As The Ramones kicked into their anthem 'Blitzkrieg Bop', the Chili Peppers wandered – naked as they day they were born – onto the side of the stage. The audience went berserk, laughing and enjoying the mayhem. Desperately trying to apologise, Flea later said that it had been their unrehearsed way of showing their admiration for the band. The Ramones were less than pleased, and went apeshit with the band after the show. Their manager tore them to pieces in the dressing room (given the state of their nakedness, it could hardly be called a 'dressing down'), calling it "the most unprofessional thing (he had) ever seen in his life." The rest of The Ramones looked on in disgust. Barely able to keep their faces straight, the Chili Peppers gazed guiltily to where their shoes would have been had they been wearing them, and showed as much remorse as they could muster. Until – as Thompson puts it – "Joey Ramone, standing quietly off to one side spoke up. 'Actually I thought it was rather amusing!'"

From then on the two bands had a friendly rapport, with Frusciante in particular developing a friendship with Johnny. It was John that brought the opportunity of being a part of the tribute album into the studio, and he who developed the slow, bluesy version of the song that appeared. Joey Ramone died of cancer in April 2001, and 'brother' Dee Dee passed away as a result of what appeared to be an accidental overdose a little over a year later.

'Universally Speaking' was released as a single album in summer 2003. A variety of editions were released, each including a selection of live or alternative tracks. Dick Rude was called in at the very last minute to direct the video for 'Universally Speaking,' with little more than a day's warning! As a result, the hilarious video is one of the band's best, and a favourite with both band and fans: it picks up with Dave Sheridan's taxi driver from the 'By The Way' video, and follows him as he goes through hell and high water to get into a Chili Pepper's gig to return to Anthony the book that he left in his cab after Dave kidnapped him! Once again an oblique reference to The Germs. The cab driver – after sniffing discarded boots, making out with an over-sized lady, and a host of other antics – finally hides away in a trash can, getting dragged to a point where he can get underneath the stage. From here he suddenly leaps up and joins in the dancing of Flea and the bouncing of Anthony on stage, a neat parody of the usual Springsteen-style 'fan-on-stage' rock video routine. A comic masterpiece and a clip that was rotated on MTV and all its competitor stations for months after the single had left the charts worldwide.

'Fortune Faded,' released as a single in November, held the crown as the best-selling rock single for several weeks in the UK chart. The Peppers were becoming more and more a successful chart-orientated singles band, again without compromising on quality. The single bore two non-album tracks as 'b-sides': 'Eskimo' and 'Bunker Hill', while a second edition of the single carried a remix of 'Californication' and the previously un-released 'Tuesday Night In Berlin'. The video of 'Californication' was nominated for 'Best Video' at the MTV awards, alongside offerings from D'Angelo, Blink 182 and N-SYNC. Perhaps inevitably, they were all pipped to the post by Eminem, and 'The Real Slim Shady.' Shame, as the promo had perhaps been the Chili Peppers most experimental effort so far in that format. Jonathan Dayton and Valerie Faris' video was a masterpiece of animation, a Playstation game ahead of the game industry's actual standards. Dayton and Faris had games and prototypes shipped over from Japan, and produced the piece at a time when PS2 was not even available in The United States. The band were fascinated by the process that turned them from human beings to computer-animated figures, subjecting themselves to a rigorous process of filming and sampling of their images. The result was more than worth it. The clip shows the animated versions of all four members of the band coming to Los Angeles from different locations – and by different means – across California. Chad snowboards over the Golden Gate Bridge. Anthony swims through a shark – and babe – infested ocean and drives a car with the licence plate 'GERMS.' John – his love for Leonardo da Vinci made evident in the clip – arrives on one of Leonardo's prototype flying machines.

The video is filled with wonderful details that enhance the reality of the gaming experience – each band members' traits appear on a side panel, for instance, listing their scores for things such as strength, stamina and agility (they all score highly!). Footage of the band playing against fast-moving, turbulent skies complements the effect, the scars on John's arms from his years of heroin abuse clearly and painfully visible. As the film comes to its conclusion and LA descends into nightmarish collapse, the band members descend to the centre of the earth as a huge earthquake centred on Hollywood opens the ground beneath them. At this point they revert to their own human selves. The imagery is clear: 'californication' of the world is a superficial (gaming) process, leading ultimately to collapse. By escaping the collapse and getting to 'the core' of things, we find our real selves. Either that or the guys were just having a ball...

In June, half way through the 2003 tour, Flea announced on the official band website that during the few weeks off the road that they had managed to sneak, they planned to write and record two new tracks for a forthcoming Greatest Hits package. Two months later, Flea described the fifteen tracks laid down as "among the most diverse and dynamic good-feeling shit we have ever done." The compilation was released in November, with new tracks 'Fortune Faded' – the next single – accompanied by 'Save The Population'. The album was also released in a DVD version that included fifteen videos and a band commentary. Interestingly, the album focussed strongly on the latter years of the Chili Peppers' career, clearly happy to represent them as tunesmith rockers of the twenty-first rather than funk monsters of the twentieth. And there's nothing wrong with that – *By The Way* and *Californication* were both landmark achievements, and there is no reason why the band shouldn't celebrate the fact.

Live At Slane Castle, the celebratory video/DVD of this mammoth event in Eire was released on the same day. This splendid collection finally caught on tape the essence of what the Chili Peppers were all about live. Concentrating on material from *Bloodsugar...* onwards, the video showcases stylish 'time-slice' footage (as used in *The Matrix*), the band hot and heavy in front of a huge audience at this Dublin venue where everyone from U2 to David Bowie had pulled off memorable, career-topping gigs.

Slane Castle was a classic example of exactly why the Chili Peppers could claim absolute aristocracy in the rock world, a key moment thankfully saved for prosperity on this DVD released in 2003. It was perhaps the one defining live moment of their career, when everything they had been through, everything they had fought to survive and everything they wanted to represent all came together in one cataclysmic gig.

RED HOT CHILI PEPPERS

As the afternoon slid into a grey Irish evening Flea, John and Chad walked on stage to the ecstatic roar of tens of thousands of fans, many of whom had travelled huge distances to attend. Like many bands, the Chili Peppers have a core audience that will fly the Atlantic or the Irish Sea as many times as it takes to follow their idols. The band seemed never to have lost that individual-care aspect of their fans, the very human touch that had attracted John in those smoky LA clubs all those years before. If 80,000 other people jumped up and down alongside you, you were still 'in there' with the band.

The wall of sound as they struck the first few notes split the Irish air – John's machine-gun guitar shattering the spaces in-between Flea's bass notes. As Kiedis joined the band the audience involvement was phenomenal, and it seemed at that moment that everyone in Ireland must have bought *By The Way* and learned the words off by heart. John's backing vocals demonstrate what a fabulous performer he had become in the years since his rehabilitation. With Anthony – long, red shorts freeing up his frenetic bouncing and pacing around the stage – John proved a complete draw to the eye. His guitar playing too showed just what it was that made this band shimmer and shake so resplendently: the tracks rocked like fuck. The influence of Hendrix was clear, not least in that cool Chili Pepper fat-Strat sound.

Hendrix's eminent skill was one of timing. He never ever lost sight of the sound he made, and knew more than any other guitarist before or since when to change it. One commentator noted after his death that Jimi could play guitar that others could never dream of achieving *while he sang at the same time*. At the risk of appalling the traditionalists, John's playing was by now approaching Hendrix's standard. Unlike so many other rock guitarists, his rhythm style is not simply to chop on alongside the bass and drums while the singer does the work until its time for another solo. John is a delicate, sensitive guitarist, and Slane Castle showed this off to the *n*-th degree. Yet when he does shove the guitar into top gear and slams his foot to the floor it is an electric moment.

Slane Castle demonstrated how important silence is in the Peppers' armoury by now too. Flea's frantic nodding and John's grinning, growling prowls around the stage were interspersed with wonderful moments of syncopated silence when all three players and Anthony too would stop dead for a split second before re-launching their juggernaut assault. All those years of jamming showed in every second they played.

By the time the band hit 'Universally Speaking', the crowd was almost demented. Chad, baseball hat to the rear of his nodding-donkey head, hit the beat simple and true. John's plain guitar chords restrained beneath Anthony's yearning vocal. Recent songs set the crowd alight – it was clear that the band's decision to promote newer material on their recent hits collection was not simply a plot to re-market recent albums: these were songs that had struck a deep core feeling in their fans. 'The Zephyr Song' was another case in point here. Flea's skeleton legs marched on the spot, his puckish face screwed up in concentration, as the front row of the audience sent waves of energy back through the crowd until the raking spotlights trained on them all showed a biblical mass of arm-waving lovers and friends. They're known as funky rockers with awesome power. But the Chili Peppers at Slane Castle could raise a tear or two with every moment of these lyrical, melancholic songs, reminding everyone of the band's turbulent journey to this point of collective joy.

Between songs it was Flea who did much of the talking. Anthony punched the mic stand around, an athletic stepson of Iggy Pop with a command of the stage second to none. The band worked through the set like a gang of railroad builders. By 'Can't Stop' the night was truly upon them, and the darkness allowed the giant video screens both behind and on either side of the stage to shine in full glory. Close-ups of the band on the sides and video footage behind to accompany each song were as much a part of the show as the guys themselves. With an exquisite sense of control, they quietened down for John's shimmering, Bob Fripp-like intro to 'Venice Queen' which built up excitement and then plunged into a version of 'Californication' that seemed to carry a lot of Anthony's emotions for his homeland with it. John, bare-chested, sat at the very edge of the stage with his legs dangling, mugged a grin, and wandered into 'Under The Bridge' - for all the world as though the sixty thousand backing vocalists were camped out in his front room. It was a sparkling moment. Arms aloft, the audience carried this wonderful night to its battering conclusion, a Flea-driven 'Power of Equality."

In particular, Slane Castle demonstrated the love the audience clearly bears for John Frusciante, and highlighted Flea's inescapable passion for entertaining. A few years earlier, Flea had said he bought into "the show-biz aesthetic of giving a dazzling performance." Dressed in a black and white skeleton suit, Flea's onstage antics – bouncing, hopping, jumping, stamping, running on the spot, shaking his head like a man possessed by demons – it is impossible to take one's eyes off him. It illustrates the dynamic of the band extremely well: it frees Kiedis as front man, taking much of the immediate audience attention from him. Released from the immediate spotlight, Anthony is more able to inject light and darkness into his performance. The band call our attentions every which way, so we never get bored watching. "Standing in one place and playing isn't what the Red Hot Chili Peppers are about," continued Flea. "...no-one would have liked Charlie Chaplin if he hadn't fallen on his face every once in a while.

If anyone wondered what the Red Hot Chili Peppers were all about, Slane Castle was a landmark show that silenced the doubters a thousand times over.

By 2004, The Red Hot Chili Peppers were amongst the top-grossing acts in the entire music industry. With *By The Way* and their *Greatest Hits* package selling vast quantities globally, they grossed more than $20 million in ticket sales alone from the ensuing tour and were listed at number 41 in the '2004 Rock Rich List'. Staggeringly, although it was no surprise that the Rolling Stones topped the list yet again, the top ten names in the list included Cher (a seemingly endless farewell tour), Simon & Garfunkel, Bon Jovi, Metallica and The Eagles. The Chilis were one place above Pearl Jam and a few ahead of Paul McCartney. An older list perhaps, which suggested that growing old in a band could be very profitable, although it was disappointing not to see younger, fresher acts not included in the list. That said, compared to some of the acts above them in the list, the Chili Peppers were spring chickens, but Kiedis wasn't worried at how long his band had lasted. He was comfortable with his status as one of rock's surviving godfathers: "The underlying love we have for one another is very powerful, and it's always there... we're in a good place as a band, we've been together for a long time and cut through a lot of bullshit."

John Frusciante released his fourth solo album in February 2004, a project that – like much of his previous solo work – had been born alongside Chili Peppers material. *Shadows Collide With People* was described by one critic as 'Wilson-esque Cali-pop,' less hooky than the Peppers' own recordings but greeted with more enthusiasm than any of his previous solo work to date. Frusciante's songwriting on his fourth solo outing is more sophisticated than on earlier collections, his blending of more traditional song structures with experimental sound more palatable. That experimental thing was still there though, but it is safe to say that by its release (compared with when he put out *Niandra Lades...*) there was a more open attitude in the market place for investigational music. Radiohead had proven with their abrasive but brilliant album *Kid A* that mainstream musicians could be allowed to wander off the musical tracks with a rucksack and a thermos flask, just as long as somewhere along the journey they called home. The album is captivating to listen to, and tracks such as 'Water', 'Second Walk' and 'The Cold' are eminently danceable.

'Carvel', the opener, seems to set the tone of the album with its ambient, bubbling textures, but its rich melody and rockier-than-ever format clearly signals that this is more of a rounded work than John's previous albums. And he appears to have had *fun* in the making of it. Bicycle Thief's Josh Klinghoffer adds bass and drums, even guesting on vocals on 'Omission', another haunting melody. If it appeared a safe route for John to take to some ears – especially those who had stuck by John's previous solo albums religiously – then for many listeners it was the first time they had heard John truly solo, and as a result it sold well. The profile now enjoyed by the rest of the members of the band meant that there was a huge potential audience of listeners who had never heard of *Niandre Lades...* never mind heard the actual album.

The album received a three star profile in *Rolling Stone*, and a rave review in *The Times*, who made it their album of the week and gave it a 3/3 rating. Frusciante talked of how he still – after all these years – didn't want to be an MTV solo artist, racking up gold discs and hitting the high points of the charts. "I'm not interested in forcing my music on people, and that's what the whole music industry nowadays is based on," he told Evan Chase of *Scene Point Blank*. Almost like the disturbed, broken-down John of old, he was still keen to stress that his work with the Chili Peppers comes out of the same creative head-basket that his solo work does, and that if he has to appear differently in the Chili Pepper world than he does in his own, then that is a part of his job that he can't avoid.

Many listeners picked 'Regret' as their favourite track, and across the album Frusciante sings with far greater confidence and – it has to be said – with more success, than previously. Chad and Flea add a richness to the trademark 'textures' of John's guitar and keyboards throughout, and the production quality is infinitely higher than on his previous solo outings. For some listeners, John had actually 'finished' a solo album, in the sense that he took the writing, playing and production to a permanent state of completion. His previous ex-Chili albums had great ideas, showed some remarkable playing or arranging, or were astonishingly bleak in their nakedness. Here, for probably the first time, he let each element of the record mature and grow at a pace where it slotted into place with every other element. It was like the difference between the fun and excitement of looking at a half-finished jigsaw puzzle that you knew you could finish, and the satisfaction of sitting back with arms folded when the puzzle *was* complete. On *Shadows* it can be said that Frusciante had the last piece of the jigsaw finally in place.

John has also made acoustic and vinyl-edition versions of *Shadows Collide With People*. He told fans that the response he had had at live gigs to acoustic versions of the songs told him that this was something his fans really wanted to hear. He stripped away all the 'production' – in essence the overdubs – and re-recorded the songs in his own home on a little eight-track cassette machine. It was touching to see John so evidently in touch both with his fans and with his work, able – despite the enormous profile of his band – to work at a 'kitchen table' level still.

In 2004 Frusciante, his long hair cut short and neat, was working with Fugazi bass player Joe Lally on a project to be released later in the year under the name Attaxia. He has been recording with Brian Eno, who came to a show after which the two got together to chew the cud, play a few tracks together and look at future projects, including Eno working on guitar tracks that John has previously recorded. Eno's work with Robert Fripp on seminal early Seventies albums like *Evening Star* and *No Pussyfooting* suggest that any released material between the former Roxy knob twiddler and guitar genius Frusciante will be nothing short of fascinating.

In 2004, the band was nominated as 'Californian Favourites' at the 27th gathering of the California Music Awards. They continued to win awards around the world, including two 'Porin' awards in Croatia, for the best foreign song ('Fortune Faded') and best foreign music DVD ('Live At Slane Castle.') Dates were announced for yet another globe-trotting tour in 2004, with Groove Armada, the Pixies and The Thrills listed early on as being among the support acts. The band were also rumoured to have been approached to play a gig for the future King of Denmark, who was due to get married in May. Prince Frederick is apparently a huge Chili Pepper fan...

CHAPTER 21

As the Red Hot Chili Peppers face the future, they can reflect on a past that is more complicated than almost any other contemporary rock band. Inevitably, this involves their missing comrade, Hillel Slovak. They say that they are thinking of him every day and with every band triumph, they wish he was there to share it, like he had been all those years ago. "If Hillel could look down and see what we were doing today," said Anthony to VH-1, "he would be proud and incredibly happy for us, because he never really got to experience this aspect of the dream, I think he'd be down for it."

The spirit of this band carries a remarkably sharp blade that cuts through bullshit like no other. Ferried around the globe in private jets, staying in the world's best hotels, they are nevertheless as punk at heart as when they started out. "My feelings are still pretty fucking intense," Flea says. "I feel I've deepened and learned to deal with my anger and put it in a better place."

"Just when you think life really sucks, you turn the corner and there's something really beautiful waiting for you, and just when you think you're on easy street and you turn the corner and there's something devastating waiting for you. I feel like we're just getting started…"

DISCOGRAPHY

Albums

The Red Hot Chili Peppers
EMI, 1984
Men Don't Kill Coyotes / Baby Appeal / Buckle Down / Get Up And Jump /
Why Don't You / Mommy Where's Daddy / Out In L.A./ Police Helicopter / You
Always Sing / Grand Pappy Du Plenty

Freaky Styley
EMI, 1985
Jungle Man / Hollywood / American Ghost Dance / If You Want Me To Stay /
Nevermind / Freaky Styley / Blackeyed Blonde / The Brother's Cup / Battleship /
Lovin' And Touchin' / Catholic School Girls Rule / Sex Rap / Thirty Dirty Birds /
Yertle The Turtle

The Uplift Mofo Party Plan
EMI, 1987
Fight Like A Brave / Funky Crime / Me & My Friends / Backwoods / Skinny
Sweaty Man / Behind The Sun / Subterranean Homesick Blues / Special Secret
Song Inside (Party On Your Pussy) / No Chump Love Sucker / Walkin' On Down
The Road / Love Trilogy / Organic Anti Beat Box Band

Mother's Milk
EMI, 1989
Good Time Boys / Higher Ground (Wonders Cover) / Subway To Venus / Magic
Johnson / Nobody Weird Like Me / Knock Me Down / Taste The Pain / Stone
Cold Bush / Fire / Pretty Little Ditty / Punk Rock Classic / Sexy Mexican Maid /
Johnny, Kick A Hole In The Sky

Blood Sugar Sex Magik
Warner Bros, 1991
The Power Of Equality / If You Have To Ask / Breaking The Girl / Funky Monks
/ Suck My Kiss / I Could Have Lied / Mellowship Slinky In B Major / The
Righteous And The Wicked / Give It Away / Blood Sugar Sex Magik / Under The
Bridge / Naked In The Rain / Apache Rose Peacock / The Greeting Song / My
Lovely Man / Sir Psycho Sexy / They're Red Hot

What Hits?
EMI, 1992
Higher Ground / Fight Like A Brave / Behind The Sun / Me & My Friends /
Backwoods / True Men Don't Kill Coyotes / Fire / Get Up And Jump / Knock
Me Down / Under The Bridge / Show Me Your Soul / If You Want Me To Stay /
Hollywood / Jungle Man / The Brother's Cup / Taste The Pain / Catholic School
Girls Rule / Johnny Kick A Hole In The Sky

One Hot Minute
Warner Bros, 1995
Warped / Aeroplane / Deep Kick / My Friends / Coffee Shop / Pea / One Big
Mob / Walkabout / Tearjerker / One Hot Minute / Falling Into Grace / Shallow
Be Thy Name / Transcending

RED HOT CHILI PEPPERS

Californication
Warner Bros, 1999
Around The World / Parallel Universe / Scar Tissue / Other Side / Get On Top / Californication / Easily / Porcelain / Emit Remmus / I Like Dirt / This Velvet Glove / Savior / Purple Stain / Right On Time / Road Trippin'

By The Way
Warner Bros, 2002
By The Way / Universally Speaking / This Is The Place / Dosed / Don't Forget Me / The Zephyr Song / Can't Stop / I Could Die For You / Midnight / Throw Away Your Television / Cabron / Tear / On Mercury / Minor Thing / Warm Tape / Venice Queen

Greatest Hits
Warner Bros, 2003
Under The Bridge / Give It Away / Californication / Scar Tissue / Soul To Squeeze / Otherside / Suck My Kiss / By The Way / Parallel Universe / Breaking The Girl / My Friends / Higher Ground / Universally Speaking / Road Trippin' / Fortune Faded / Save The Population

Singles And Eps

Unbridled Funk And Roll 4 Your Soul
EMI, 1989
Taste The Pain / Millionaires Against Hunger / Castles Made Of Sand / Higher Ground (Daddy-O Mix)

Hollywood
EMI, 1985
Hollywood (Africa) (Extended Dance Mix) / Hollywood (Africa) (Dub Mix) / Nevermind

Fight Like A Brave
EMI , 1987
Higher Ground / Fight Like A Brave (Mofo Mix)
Or
Fight Like A Brave (Mofo Mix) / Fight Like A Brave (Knucklehead Mix) / Fire

Abbey Road E.P.
EMI, 1988
Fire / Backwoods / Catholic School Girls Rule / Hollywood (Africa) / True Men Don't Kill Coyotes

Knock Me Down
EMI, 1989
Knock Me Down / Punk Rock Classic / Pretty Little Ditty

Higher Ground
EMI 1989
Higher Ground / Higher Ground (Munckin Mix) / Millionaires Against Hunger /

Mommy Where's Daddy
Or
Higher Ground / Fight Like A Brave / Behind The Sun Out In L.A.

Taste The Pain
EMI, 1990
Taste The Pain / Show Me Your Soul / Castles Made Of Sand (Live)

Suck My Kiss
Warner Bros, 1992
Suck My Kiss / Search And Destroy / Fela's Cock

Breaking The Girl
Warner Bros, 1992
Breaking The Girl (Edit)'Fela´S Cock / Suck My Kiss (Live) / I Could Have
Lied (Live)

Behind The Sun
Warner Bros, 1992
Behind The Sun Higher Ground (Pearly 12") / If You Want Me To Stay (Pink
Mustang Mix) / Knock Me Down

Give It Away
Warner Bros, 1993
Give It Away (Single Mix) / Give It Away (12" Mix) / Search & Destroy / Give
It Away (Rasta Mix) / Give It Away (Album Version)

Under The Bridge
Warner Bros, 1993
Under The Bridge / Give It Away

If You Have To Ask
Warner Bros, 1993
If You Have To Ask (Radio Edit) / If You Have To Ask (Disco Krisco Mix) / If
You Have To Ask (Scott & Garth Mix) / Give It Away (Edit)

Warped
Warner Bros, 1995
Warped / Pea / Melancholy Mechanics

My Friends
Warner Bros, 1995
My Friends / Coffee Shop / Let's Make Evil (Non Lp Track) / Stretch (Non LP
Track)

Aeroplane
Warner Bros, 1996
Aeroplane (Clean Edit) / Backwoods (Live) / Transcending (Live) / Me & My
Friends

RED HOT CHILI PEPPERS

Scar Tissue
Warner Bros, 1999
Scar Tissue / Gong Li / Instrumental #1

Around The World
Warner Bros, 1999
Around The World / Parallel Universe (Live) / Teatro Jam / Me & My Friends

Otherside
Warner Bros, 1999
Otherside / How Strong / My Lovely Man (Live) / Road Trippin' (No Strings Version)

Californication
Warner Bros, 2000
Californication / End Of Show Brisbane (Live Jam) / End Of Show State College (Live Jam) / I Could Have Lied Live

Road Trippin'
Warner Bros, 2000
Road Trippin' (Album Version) / Californication (Live) / Blood Sugar Sex Magik (Live) / Under The Bridge (Live)

By The Way
Warner Bros, 2002
By The Way / Time (New Non-Album Track) / Search And Destroy (Live) / Teenager In Love (New Non-Album Track) / What Is Soul (Live)

The Zephyr Song
Warner Bros, 2002
The Zephyr Song / Body Of Water / Someone / Out Of Range / Rivers Of Avalon

Can't Stop
Warner Bros, 2003
Can't Stop / If You Have To Ask (Live) / Christ Church Fireworks Music (Live) / Right On Time (Live) / Nothing To Lose (Live)

Universally Speaking
Warner Bros, 2003
Universally Speaking / Slowly Deeply / Universally Speaking (Video)

Fortune Faded
Warner Bros, 2003
Fortune Faded / Californication (Remixed by Ekkehard Ehelers) / Tuesday Night In Berlin (Non LP Track)

How Strong
Warner Bros, 2004
How Strong / Otherside

Boxsets and Best Of

Rare - E.P.
Warner Bros, 1991
Soul To Squeeze / Fela's Cock / Sikamikanico / Search And Destroy

Live Rare Remix Box
Warner Bros, 1994
Give It Away (Live) / Nobody Wierd Like Me (Live) / Suck My Kiss (Live) / I Could Have Lied (Live)

Out In L.A.
Warner Bros, 1994
Remixed and Unreleased Demo tracks Compilation
higher Ground (12"Voc. Mix) / Hollywood (Extended Dance Mix) / If You Want Me To Dance / Behind The Sun Ben Grosse Remix / Castles Made Of Sand (Live) / special Secret Song Inside (Live) / F.u.- Live / Get Up And Jump / Out In L.A. / Green Heaven / Police Helicopter / Nevermind / Sex Rap / Blues For Meister / You Always Sing The Same / Stranded / Flea Fly / What It Is / Deck The Halls (prev. unrel.)

Essential Red Hot Chili Peppers:
Under The Covers
EMI, 1998
They're Red Hot / Fire / Subterranean Homesick Blues / Higher Ground / If You Want Me To Stay / Why Don't You Love Me / Tiny Dancer (Live) / Castles Made Of Sand (Live) / Dr. Funkenstein (Live) / Hollywood / Search & Destroy / Higher Ground / Hollywood (Africa) (Extended Dance Mix)

The Original Series
Warner Bros, 1998
Boxed Set
Jungle Man / Hollywood / American Ghost Dance / If You Want Me To Stay / Nevermind / Freakey Styley / Blackeyed Blonde / Brothers Cup, The / Battle Ship / Lovin' And Touchin' / Catholic School Girls Rule / Sex Rap / Thirty Dirty Birds / Yertle The Turtle / Fight Like A Brave / Funky Crime / Me & My Friends / Backwoods / Skinny Sweaty Man / Behind The Sun / Subterranean Homesick Blues / Special Secret Song Inside / No Chump Love Sucker / Walkin' On Down The Road / Love Trilogy / Organic Anti-Beat Box Band / True Men Don't Kill Coyotes / Baby Appeal / Buckle Down / Get Up And Jump / Why Don't You Love Me / Green Heaven / Mommy Where's Daddy? / Out In L.A. / Police Helicopter / You Always Sing / Grand Pappy Du Plenty

Bootlegs

Anthoney's Penis - Loreley Open Air Festival, Loreley, Goarshausen, Germany 17/08/85
Disc 1 - Out In L.A. / Jungle Man / Buckle Down / Green Heaven / Hollywood (Africa) / Stranded / Black Eyed Blonde / Baby Appeal /You Always Sing The Same / True Men Don't Kill Coyotes / Get Up And Jump / Battle Ship / Fire (Jimi Hendrix)
Disc 2 - Out In L.A. / Buckle Down / Jungle Man / Back Woods / Black Eyed Blonde / Anarchy In U.K. / Green Heaven / Nervous Breakdown / Police Helicopter / Baby Appeal / Theme From 'Rocky' / Get Up, Stand Up (Bob Marley) / Me & My Friends / Catholic School Girls Rule / Special Secret Song Inside / Locomotion / We Got New Job, Load! / Get Up And Jump / Nevermind / Yertle The Turtle / Foxy Lady

Seattle, USA, 02/05/86
Out In LA / Buckle Down / Jungle Man / Baby Appeal / Black Eyed Blonde / American Ghost Dance / Green Heaven / Police Helicopter / 3 Dirty Birds / Mommy Where's Daddy / Catholic School Girls Rule / Weird Version Of Sex Rap / Hollywood / True Men Don't Kill Coyotes / Nevermind / Fire / You Always Sing The Same / Yertle The Turtle / Funkenstein / Freaky Styley / Behind The Sun / Neutron Bomb

What The Funk? Demos & Outtakes 1985-1988
Subterranean Homesick Blues (Bob Dylan) / Me And My Friends / Backwoods / Party On Your Pussy / Love Trilogy / Iiinstrumental #1 / Instrumental #2 / On My Way To Town / Da Da Is Not Dead / Leadbelly / Foxy Lady (Jimi Hendrix) / Instrumental #3 / Skinny Sweaty Man / Instrumental #4 / Instrumental #5 / Instrumental #6 / If You Want Me To Stay Part 1 / If You Want Me To Stay Part 2 / If You Want Me To Stay Part 3 / Party On Your Pussy (Jam)

Push To Flush - Brussels, Belgium, 1988
Out In L.A. / Organic Anti-Beat Box Band / Heartbreaker (Led Zeppelin) / Me And My Friends / Fight Like A Brave / Blackeyed Blonde / Love Trilogy / Hollywood (Africa) / Police Helicopter / Party On Your Pussy / Whole Lotta Love (Led Zeppelin) / Back In Black (AC/DC) / Backwoods / Subterranean Homesick Blues (Bob Dylan) / Anarchy In The U.K. (Sex Pistols) / Skinny Sweaty Man / No Chump Love Sucker / Mommy Where's Daddy / Get Up And Jump / Magic Johnson / Nevermind / Battle Ship / Yertle The Turtle / Freaky Styley Medley / Neverious Breakdown (Black Flag) / Fire (Jimi Hendrix)

Christmas Party - San Diego, USA 19/12/91
Love Trilogy / Organic Anti Beat Box Band / Bullet Proof / Suck My Kiss / Blackeyed Blonde / Funky Crime / Give It Away / Nobody Weird Like Me / Stone Cold Bush / If You Have To Ask / Blood Sugar Sex Magic / Magic Johnson / I Could Have Lied / Subway To Venus / Funky Time Squel / Special Secret Song Inside / Me And My Friends / Yertle The Turtle / Crosstown Traffic (Jimi Hendrix)

Lollapalooza 92, New Orleans, LA 04/09/92
Suck My Kiss / Subterranean Homesick Blues (Bob Dylan) / My Lovely Man / Nobody Weird Like Me / If You Have To Ask / Stone Cold Bush / Blood Sugar Sex Magik / Higher Ground (Stevie Wonder) / Magic Johnson / Under The Bridge / Party On Your Pussy / The Needle And The Damage Done (Neil Young) / Me And My Friends / Mommy Where's Daddy / Crosstown Traffic (Jimi Hendrix)

Woodstock '94 - Saugerties, NY, USA 14/08/94
Give It Away / Suck My Kiss / Warped / Stone Cold Bush / If You Have To Ask / Organic Anti-Beat Box Band / Aeroplane / Blood Sugar Sex Magik / Pea / My Lovely Man / Higher Ground / Under The Bridge / Me & My Friends / The Power Of Equality

Gravity - Live at The Entertainment Centre, Sydney, Australia May 15th 1996
The Power Of Equality / Warped / Suck My Kiss / Walkabout / Blood Sugar Sex Magik / My Friends / Jesus! / Higher Ground / Pea / Shallow Be Thy Game / Aeroplane / One Big Mob / Under The Bridge / Give It Away / Deep Kick / Coffee Shop

KBLT (Pirate Radio Station) - Los Angeles, 01/06/98 + John Frusciante - Rarities
How Could I Love Myself (Flea) / Skinny Sweaty Man / Jam / I Could Have Lied / Not Great Men / Ten To Butter Blood Voodoo / Untitled #11 / Love Them So (Flea) / It Could Have Been / Police Helicopter / Soul To Squeeze / Nervous Breakdown / Usually Just A T-Shirt / Ants / Outside Space / Unknown / Untitled #11 / Tiny Dancer / Inca Roads / Under The Bridge (SNL) / Under The Bridge (Acoustic) / Castles Made Of Sand / Crosstown Traffic / Dr. Funkenstein / Search And Destroy / Soul To Squeeze / Sikamikanico

One Hot Weekend I - Las Vegas, NV, 05/09/98
Dirt / Under The Bridge / Backwoods / Bunker Hill / If You Have To Ask / I Want You Back (Jackson 5) / Fat Man (Flea W/Clara) / Blackeyed Blonde / Emit Remmus / I Could Have Lied / Give It Away / Tiny Dancer (Elton John) / Scar Tissue / Me & My Friends / Pea (Flea Solo) / Soul To Squeeze / Power Of Equality / Yertle The Turtle / Freaky Styley / 1970 (Iggy Pop)

One Hot Weekend II - Las Vegas, NV, 06/09/98
Dirt / Funky Crime / Under The Bridge / Bunker Hill / If You Have To Ask / I Want You Back (Jackson 5) / Nobody Weird Like Me / Emit Remmus / Fat Man (Flea W/Clara) / Long Division (Fugazi) / Give It Away / Your Song (Elton John) / Scar Tissue / Love Trilogy / Pea (Flea Solo) / Soul To Squeeze / Me & My Friends / Yertle The Turtle / Freaky Styley / Search And Destroy (Iggy Pop)

Red Hot & Bizarre - Bizarre Festival, Cologne, Germany, 20/08/99
Around The World / Give It Away / Scar Tissue / Suck My Kiss / Soul To Squeeze / I Like Dirt / If You Have To Ask / Organic Anti-Beat Box Band / My Lovely Man / Right On Time / Under The Bridge / Me & My Friends / Yertle Trilogy / Cosmic Slop

Big Day Out - Sydney, Australia, 26/01/00
Around The World / Give It Away / Untitled #11 / Crowd Trouble / Scar Tissue / Suck My Kiss / If You Have To Ask / Otherside / Skinny Sweaty Man / Your Pussy Is Glued To A Building On Fire / I Could Have Lied / Easily / Californication / Right On Time / Under The Bridge / Me And My Friends / Soul To Squeezee / Power Of Equality

INDEX

F

H

I

J

M